WALKING
BERLIN

WALKING
BERLIN

THE BEST OF THE CITY

Paul Sullivan

NATIONAL GEOGRAPHIC
Washington, D.C.

WALKING BERLIN

CONTENTS

PART 1

PAGE 12
WHIRLWIND TOURS

PART 2

PAGE 46
BERLIN'S NEIGHBORHOODS

PART 3

PAGE 172
TRAVEL ESSENTIALS

Previous pages: Alexanderplatz. Left: Hackesche Höfe. Right: Statue at Jagdschloss Grunewald. Above right: East Side Gallery. Bottom right: Reichstag

Introduction

I moved to Berlin almost 20 years ago for the cheap rents and edgy art, music scene, and relaxed vibe. Equally important: I was excited to live in a place where past and present collide everywhere you look.

Few cities have lived as many lives as Berlin. In a scant century, the city's been an imperial capital, a synonym for decadence, and a Nazi stronghold. Bombed, invaded, and occupied, then suddenly divided, unexpectedly reunited, and once again made the capital of a unified Germany.

You can see it all on Unter den Linden, the avenue that runs through the heart of the city's eastern half. Start under the TV tower, an East German icon. In the park below, snap a selfie with statues of Marx and Engels, the architects of a system Germans eagerly discarded more than 30 years ago. Head west past the Habsburg-era Berlin Cathedral, still scarred by the bombs of World War II, and Humboldt University, where Albert Einstein once taught. Pass through the famous Brandenburg Gate—used as a triumphal arch by Napoleon and Hitler—and cross over the narrow line of bricks that marks the course of the Berlin Wall. Finally, take in the glittering glass dome atop the stolid gray stone of the Reichstag.

Locals relax over a glass of Berliner Pilsner in the leafy Schleusenkrug beer garden in the city's popular Tiergarten park.

Using this guide, remember: The German capital is no museum, though it has plenty of them. Three decades after the fall of the Berlin Wall, the city has become an oasis for creative types of every stripe. Berlin's intriguing, often difficult history hasn't kept it from embracing the present and pursuing the future.

Andrew Curry
National Geographic Traveler *writer and Berlin-based foreign correspondent*

Visiting Berlin

Since the fall of the Wall in 1989, Berlin has undergone a rapid, yet considered, program of regeneration. Focused on the historical center, the once-divided city is now whole again. What you see is a thriving cultural capital that nevertheless remains studded with fascinating glimpses into its turbulent past.

Berlin in a Nutshell

Berlin's historic center straddles the Spree River, which flows from east to west through the city. Radiating out from here are a number of neighborhoods, each with its own distinct characteristics. They include buzzy Kreuzberg to the south, gritty Friedrichshain to the east, and leafy Tiergarten to the west. Each of these neighborhoods—and others featured in this book—offers a diverse range of sights and is well worth a day's visit in its own right. Much of what now makes up central Berlin lies behind the Berlin Wall in the former German Democratic Republic (GDR)—in German, the Deutsche Demokratische Republik (DDR)—and remnants of the Cold War years abound.

Berlin Day-by-Day

Open every day With some exceptions for major public holidays, almost all sites are open every day.

Monday All sites open except AlliiertenMuseum, Alte Nationalgalerie, Altes Museum, Bode-Museum, Deutsches Technikmuseum, Gemäldegalerie, Jagdschloss Grunewald (year-round), Knoblauchhaus, Museum Europäischer Kulturen, Neues Museum, visitor center at Gedenkstätte Berliner Mauer.

Tuesday All sites open except Berlinische Galerie, Deutsche Kinemathek, Haus der Kulturen der Welt (exhibitions only), PalaisPopulaire.

Thursday Pergamonmuseum, Neues Museum, and Alte Nationalgalerie are open until 8 p.m.; PalaisPopulaire is open until 9 p.m.

Saturday/Sunday November through March Jagdschloss Grunewald is only open on weekends. All sites open except Temporary Bauhaus-Archiv (Sunday).

Tourists enjoy a cruise on the Spree River between Museumsinsel and Monbijoupark.

Navigating Berlin

With the vast majority of key sights in or around the historic center of Berlin, the core of the city is easily navigated on foot. There is also an extremely efficient public transportation network that makes good use of frequent buses *(Busse)*, trams *(Strassenbahnen)*, and trains. These operate both underground *(U-Bahn)* and overground *(S-Bahn)* for swift access to those sights that lie farther afield. Before setting out, arm yourself with a detailed street map of the city and its transportation network, available from Berlin's tourist authority (see p. 176–177).

Enjoying Berlin for Less

Berlin is *the* city of discounts—either on public transportation, for entry to key tourist sights, or for eating and drinking in numerous establishments. By far the best deals are to be had with the **Berlin WelcomeCard** (see p. 175), available for various lengths of stay. Cards come with free public transportation for 1 adult plus up to 3 children (aged 6 to 14). All WelcomeCards include discounts on about 180 cultural sights and restaurants, and are issued with free street maps and network plans for public transportation.

Using This Guide

Each tour—which might be only a walk, or might take advantage of the city's public transportation as well—is plotted on a map and has been planned to take into account opening hours and the times of day when sites are less crowded. Many end near restaurants or lively nightspots for evening activities.

Whirlwind Tours

Whirlwind Tours are for people who have only a day or a weekend to spend in the city and want to be sure that they see the very best. Choose your tour based on your time and interests: One Day; Weekend; For Fun; For Spies; For Contemporary Architecture Fans; and Weekend with Kids.

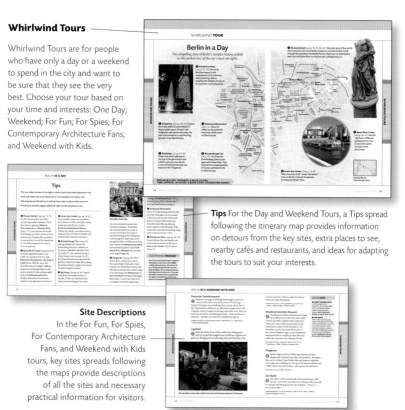

Tips For the Day and Weekend Tours, a Tips spread following the itinerary map provides information on detours from the key sites, extra places to see, nearby cafés and restaurants, and ideas for adapting the tours to suit your interests.

Site Descriptions
In the For Fun, For Spies, For Contemporary Architecture Fans, and Weekend with Kids tours, key sites spreads following the maps provide descriptions of all the sites and necessary practical information for visitors.

Neighborhood Tours

The seven neighborhood tours each begin with an introduction, followed by an itinerary map highlighting the key sites that make up the tour and detailed key sites descriptions. Each tour is followed by an "in-depth" spread showcasing one major site along the route, a "distinctly" Berlin spread providing background information on a quintessential element of that neighborhood, and a "best of" spread that groups sites thematically.

Itinerary Map A map of the neighborhood shows the locations of the key sites, U- and S-Bahn stations, and main streets.

Captions These briefly describe the key sites and give instructions on finding the next site on the tour. Page references direct you to full descriptions of the key sites on the following pages.

Route
Dotted lines link the key sites.

Price Ranges for Key Sites

€	Less than €4
€€	€4–€8
€€€	€8–€13
€€€€	€13–€18
€€€€€	More than €18

Price Ranges for Good Eats (for one person, excluding drinks)

€	Less than €15
€€	€15–€25
€€€	€25–€40
€€€€	€40–€60
€€€€€	More than €60

Key Sites Descriptions These provide a detailed description and highlights for each site, following the order on the map, plus its address, website, phone number, entrance fee, days closed, and nearest U- or S-Bahn station.

Good Eats Refer to these lists for a selection of cafés and restaurants.

PART 1

Whirlwind Tours

Berlin in a Day

The compelling story of Berlin's complex history unfolds on this packed tour of the city's must-see sights.

8 Potsdamer Platz (see pp. 56–57) Marvel at the skyscrapers in this masterpiece of 21st-century urban planning, before sampling the delights of one of its many bars and restaurants.

6 Tiergarten (see pp. 98–99) Explore the many paths of central Berlin's largest green space. Dotted with sculptures and memorials today, the park once served as a royal hunting ground. Cross Ebertstrasse.

7 Holocaust Monument (see p. 55) Pause to reflect at this powerful memorial. Walk south on Ebertstrasse.

5 Reichstag (see pp. 62–63) Follow the spiral walkway to the top of the glass dome and a bird's-eye view over Berlin. Cross Scheidemannstrasse and head into the Tiergarten.

4 Brandenburger Tor (see p. 54) You'll see the Brandenburg Gate as you approach Pariser Platz. Pass beneath the winged goddess of victory and head north on Ebertstrasse.

Map labels:
Hauptbahnhof
LUISENSTRASSE
KAPELLE-UFER
SPREEBOGEN-PARK
Bundestag
Berlin Wall Memorial
Memorial to Sinti and Roma Victims of National Socialism
Reichstag
REGIERUN...
VIERTEL
Haus der Kulturen der Welt
Brandenbu...
To Siegessäule
STRASSE DES 17. JUNI
Brandenburger Tor
Holocau... Monume...
Tiergarten 6
Memorial to Homosexuals Persecuted under Nazism
TIERGARTENTUNNEL
VOSSSTRAS...
Sony Center
LEIPZIGER PLATZ
Potsdamer Pla...
Potsdamer Platz
Potsdame... Platz
POTSDAMER STR.
MARLENE-DIETRICH-PLATZ
LINKSTRASSE
TILLA-DURIEUX-PARK
KÖTHENER STR.
STRESEM...
SCHÖNEBERGER...
ASKANISCHER PLATZ
Mendelssohn-Bartholdy-Park
MENDELSSOHN-BARTHOLDY-PARK
Anhalter Bahnhof
UFER
Gleisdreieck
Möckernbrü...

BERLIN IN A DAY DISTANCE: 6 MILES (10 KM)
TIME: APPROX. 10 HOURS S-BAHN START: HACKESCHER MARKT

WHIRLWIND TOURS

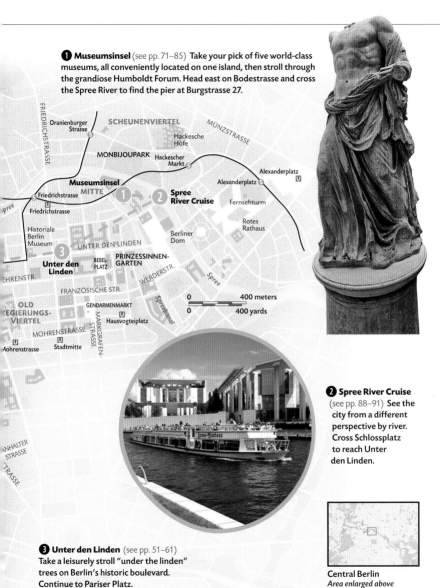

1 Museumsinsel (see pp. 71–85) Take your pick of five world-class museums, all conveniently located on one island, then stroll through the grandiose Humboldt Forum. Head east on Bodestrasse and cross the Spree River to find the pier at Burgstrasse 27.

FRIEDRICHSTRASSE

Oranienburger Strasse

SCHEUNENVIERTEL

MÜNZSTRASSE

Hackesche Höfe

MONBIJOUPARK   Hackescher Markt

Alexanderplatz

Museumsinsel   Alexanderplatz

MITTE

Friedrichstrasse   **2 Spree River Cruise**

pree   Friedrichstrasse   Fernsehturm

Historiale Berlin Museum   Rotes Rathaus

Berliner Dom

UNTER DEN LINDEN

3

Unter den Linden   BEBEL-PLATZ   PRINZESSINNEN-GARTEN

WERDERSTR.

Spree

EHRENSTR.

FRANZÖSISCHE STR.

| 0 | 400 meters |
| 0 | 400 yards |

OLD REGIERUNGS-VIERTEL   GENDARMENMARKT

Spreekanal

MOHRENSTRASSE   Hausvogteiplatz

MARKGRAFEN-STRASSE

Mohrenstrasse   Stadtmitte

ANHALTER STRASSE

TRASSE

2 Spree River Cruise (see pp. 88–91) See the city from a different perspective by river. Cross Schlossplatz to reach Unter den Linden.

Central Berlin
Area enlarged above

3 Unter den Linden (see pp. 51–61) Take a leisurely stroll "under the linden" trees on Berlin's historic boulevard. Continue to Pariser Platz.

Tips

This tour offers the best of the sights in Berlin. Each is described elsewhere in the book—just follow the cross-references for more detailed information. The following tips provide advice on visiting these major locations when you have limited time and also suggest additional sights nearby and places to eat.

❶ Museumsinsel (see pp. 71–85)
Arrive early to avoid the crowds, especially in summer. If you don't plan on getting a ■ **BERLIN WELCOMECARD** or a **MUSEUM PASS** (see p. 175), you can beat the hordes by booking your visit in advance *(www.smb.museum)*. Despite their proximity to one another, it would be exhausting to visit all five museums in a day, so focus on just one.

❷ Spree River Cruise (see pp. 88–91)
Glide through Berlin's historic city center on a one-hour boat tour with ■ **BERLINER WASSERSPORT UND SERVICE GMBH & CO.** (BWSG; see p. 88). From the water, you will get a different perspective on Museumsinsel, as well as see a number of other primary sights, such as the ■ **REGIERUNGSVIERTEL** (Berlin's ultramodern Government Quarter). Last departure is at 6:45 p.m.

❸ Unter den Linden (see pp. 51–61)
Just round the corner you can admire the collection of 19th- and 20th-century sculptures inside the neo-Gothic ■ **FRIEDRICHSWERDERSCHE KIRCHE** *(Werderscher Markt, www.smb.museum)*, designed by Karl Friedrich Schinkel and reopened after extensive renovation.

❹ Brandenburger Tor (see p. 54)
Seeking refreshment? Admire the Brandenburg Gate from a distance on the terrace of ■ **HOTEL ADLON** *(Unter den Linden 77)*, the celebrity hot spot of the Weimar years (see pp. 64–67). You'll pass the hotel as you approach the gate from Unter den Linden. If it's raining, step inside and enjoy a tipple at the hotel's decadent lounge bar instead.

❺ Reichstag (see pp. 62–63) Visitors to the dome are admitted every 15 minutes. Tickets are available for free online *(www.bundestag.de)* or on site,

Hotel Adlon, Pariser Platz

but we recommend securing your time slot in andvance. To facilitate the access procedure, be on site 15 minutes beforehand. If you plan to visit the Reichstag in the evening (see Customizing Your Day), take a stroll through the ribbon of official structures that makes up the ■ REGIERUNGSVIERTEL (Government Quarter) to find the ■ BERLIN WALL MEMORIAL, which includes some original segments.

❻ Tiergarten (see pp. 98–99) If time is short, confine your visit to the eastern flank of this park, which contains two World War II memorials. Directly across from the southern edge of the Reichstag is the ■ MEMORIAL TO SINTI AND ROMA VICTIMS OF NATIONAL SOCIALISM, a round water basin with a triangular stone stele supporting a single flower at its center. Farther south, near Lennéstrasse, is the ■ MEMORIAL TO HOMOSEXUALS PERSECUTED UNDER NAZISM (see p. 55). If you have time for a breezy stroll, pick any of the paths leading to the ■ SIEGESSÄULE (Victory Column; see p. 99) on Strasse des 17. Juni before moving on.

❼ Holocaust Monument (see p. 55) Early evening is the best time for a visit. Although it can be accessed at all hours, most tourists will have left by now. A certain stillness descends toward the end of the day, allowing you to experience the full impact of the memorial's somewhat disorienting design without distraction from others.

❽ Potsdamer Platz (see pp. 56–57) Round off your day watching the sun set from the terrace bar at the top of ■ KOLLHOFF-TOWER (*Alte Potsdamer Strasse 7*).

CUSTOMIZING **YOUR DAY**

One of the most pleasant ways to enjoy the Reichstag is to book dinner at the **Käfer** rooftop restaurant (see p. 63; *last entry 10 p.m.*). Satisfy yourself with the river view of the building in the morning and skip the Reichstag visit in the afternoon. If you take this option, it makes sense to swap the last two sights of the day. See p. 25 for more options at Potsdamer Platz.

Berlin in a Weekend

*This compact tour of Berlin's most-visited landmarks
starts with a cruise on the Spree River.*

| 0 | 400 meters |
| 0 | 400 yards |

Hauptbahnho

❶ Spree River Cruise (see pp. 88–91)
Relax on this leisurely cruise of the
city's main sights. Heading west, cross
Museumsinsel on Bodestrasse and
walk south on Am Zeughaus,
flanking the Spreekanal.

KANZLERGARTEN
Bundeskanzleramt

Haus der
Kulturen
der Welt

❷ Unter den Linden
(see pp. 51–61) Head
west on this grand
boulevard. You'll see
an equestrian statue
of Frederick the Great
on the way. With the
Brandenburg Gate in
sight, make your way
to Pariser Platz.

STRASSE DES 17. JUN

TIERGARTEN

BELLEVUEALLEE

TIERGARTENSTRASSE

**KULTUR
FORUM**

Gemälde-
galerie

Neue
National-
galerie

❸ Brandenburger Tor
(see p. 54) Pass through the gate
to Ebertstrasse, shaking hands
with the Berlin Bear if you're lucky
enough to spot him. Head south.

❹ Holocaust Monument
(see p. 55) Visit the Ort der
Information (Information Center)
at the southeastern corner of this
memorial for a sobering tribute to
the Jewish victims of the Holocaust.

**BERLIN IN A WEEKEND DAY 1 DISTANCE: 2 MILES (3.2 KM)
TIME: APPROX. 6 HOURS S-BAHN START: HACKESCHER MARKT**

WHIRLWIND TOURS

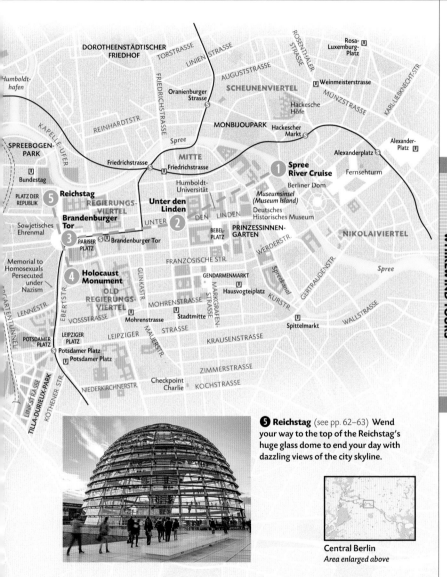

DOROTHEENSTÄDTISCHER FRIEDHOF

TORSTRASSE

LINIEN STRASSE

Humboldt-hafen

AUGUSTSTRASSE

ROSENTHALER STRASSE

Rosa-Luxemburg-Platz Ⓤ

SCHEUNENVIERTEL

FRIEDRICHSTRASSE

Oranienburger Strasse

Ⓤ Weinmeisterstrasse

MÜNZSTRASSE

KARL-LIEBKNECHT-STR.

REINHARDTSTR.

KAPELLE-UFER

Hackesche Höfe

MONBIJOUPARK

Hackescher Markt Ⓢ

SPREEBOGEN-PARK

Spree

MITTE

Ⓤ Bundestag

Friedrichstrasse

Ⓤ Friedrichstrasse

Alexanderplatz Ⓢ

Alexander-Platz Ⓤ

1 **Spree River Cruise**

Fernsehturm

PLATZ DER REPUBLIK

5 **Reichstag**

Humboldt-Universität

REGIERUNGS-VIERTEL

Berliner Dom

Brandenburger Tor

Unter den Linden

Museumsinsel (Museum Island)

Sowjetisches Ehrenmal

3 PARISER PLATZ Ⓢ Ⓤ Brandenburger Tor

UNTER

DEN LINDEN

2

BEBEL PLATZ

Deutsches Historisches Museum

PRINZESSINNEN-GARTEN

NIKOLAIVIERTEL

Memorial to Homosexuals Persecuted under Nazism

4 **Holocaust Monument**

FRANZÖSISCHE STR.

WERDERSTR.

Spree

GLINKASTR.

OLD REGIERUNGS-VIERTEL

GARTEN-TUNNEL

LENNÉSTR.

EBERTSTR.

VOSSSTRASSE

MOHRENSTRASSE

Mohrenstrasse

GENDARMENMARKT

Ⓤ Hausvogteiplatz

MARKGRAFEN-STRASSE

Stadtmitte

KURSTR.

SPREEKANAL

GERTRAUDENSTR.

WALLSTRASSE

POTSDAMER PLATZ

LEIPZIGER PLATZ

LEIPZIGER

MAUERSTR.

STRASSE

KRAUSENSTRASSE

Ⓤ Spittelmarkt

Spittelmarkt

Potsdamer Platz Ⓤ Potsdamer Platz

ZIMMERSTRASSE

LINKSTRASSE

TILLA-DURIEUX-PARK

KOTHENER STR.

NIEDERKIRCHNERSTR.

Checkpoint Charlie

KOCHSTRASSE

5 **Reichstag** (see pp. 62–63) Wend your way to the top of the Reichstag's huge glass dome to end your day with dazzling views of the city skyline.

Central Berlin
Area enlarged above

Tips

Two days in Berlin affords enough time to get a true sense of this city's incredible diversity. Day One may appear relatively relaxed, but there is plenty of scope for improvisation. Read up about these sights' main attractions later in the book and consider the following tips for interesting alternatives and detours on the way.

WHIRLWIND TOURS

❶ Spree River Cruise (see pp. 88–91) The best way to get an overview of the city in a very short time, this cruise makes an ideal start to your weekend break. Join a round-trip river cruise run by ▪ **BERLINER WASSERSPORT UND SERVICE GMBH & CO.** (BWSG; see p. 88). Boats run from 11:15 a.m. to 6:45 p.m., and cruises last an hour (but longer trips are available too). Morning cruises tend to be less busy than afternoon ones, and it is worth booking

Browsing book stalls at Humboldt University

online in advance *(www.bwsg-berlin.de)* to avoid disappointment in summer.

❷ Unter den Linden (see pp. 51-61) As you stroll from the east end of this grand boulevard to the west, seek out a couple of courtyards rarely discovered by tourists. The first is at Berlin's seat of learning, ▪ **HUMBOLDT-UNIVERSITÄT** *(No. 6)*, whose previous students include Albert Einstein and Karl Marx. On most days, you'll find locals browsing a secondhand book market held here *(times vary)*. Next door is one of the branches of the ▪ **STAATSBIBLIOTHEK ZU BERLIN** *(No. 8)*, with its courtyard that offers shady benches on which to seek a few minutes respite from the heat and the boulevard hordes in summer. If you're seeking refreshment, head to any one of a number of cafés that line the boulevard. Among Berlin's most treasured is the venerable

■ **Café Einstein** *(No. 42)*, with its classic Viennese interior and a new terrace on the boulevard. You'll find it just before the intersection with Glinkastrasse.

❸ **Brandenburger Tor** (see p. 54) The Brandenburg Gate is one of the city's most visited sights and busy at almost any time of day. If your arrival coincides with a bus tour (or two), seek a moment's peace in the less publicized ■ **Room of Silence** on the northern side of the gate. Or pass through the gate and into the ■ **Tiergarten** (see pp. 98–99) for a leafy detour through the eastern end of Berlin's largest park. A short walk on Strasse des 17. Juni will bring you to the ■ **Sowjetisches Ehrenmal** (see p. 99) commemorating the Soviet victory over the Nazis in the Battle of Berlin. Also at this end of the park—opposite the Holocaust Monument (see below)—is the ■ **Memorial to Homosexuals Persecuted under Nazism** (see p. 55). You can exit the park on Ebertstrasse to return to the tour.

❹ **Holocaust Monument** (see p. 55) The Holocaust Monument is one of the best known tourist attractions in Berlin, yet not all visitors discover the 8,600-square-foot (800 sq m) ■ **Ort der Information** (Information Center) below ground. The center features four themed rooms dedicated to more

CUSTOMIZING **YOUR DAY**

A Spree River cruise may be less appealing in the colder months, and there is a short period *(mid-Nov.–mid-March)* when there is no service. Opt instead to start the day at the **Deutsches Historisches Museum** (German Historical Museum; see p. 59) at the eastern end of Unter den Linden— to see either the permanent galleries or the museum's temporary exhibition. Alternatively, treat yourself to brunch at the nearby **Museumscafé** (see p. 68).

personal aspects of the tragedy, such as letters and heirlooms belonging to Jewish families massacred by the Nazis.

❺ **Reichstag** (see pp. 62–63) All visitors must register in advance. Instead of wasting time doing this on the day, prebook your tickets online, choosing a time slot to tie in with your itinerary. If you arrive early, the ■ **Bundeskanzleramt** (Federal Chancellery; see p. 37) is an additional architectural highlight of Berlin's Government Quarter (once a year in September it also is open to the public). For a great view of the whole quarter, cross Kanzlerbrücke (the bridge behind the Bundeskanzleramt) to ■**Kanzlergarten.** North of the Reichstag building, ■ **Spreebogenpark** (see p. 104) hugs the bend of the Spree River, providing pleasant waterfront strolling.

Berlin in a Weekend

*Explore the city's cultural highlights with this
full-on tour of central Berlin.*

❶ Hackesche Höfe (see pp. 80–81) With its eight interconnected courtyards, this elegant art nouveau development is a haven of trendy cafés and boutiques. Walk south on Neue Promenade and then Burgstrasse.

❷ Berliner Dom (see p. 75–76) Find your bearings in central Berlin from the top of the city's immense cathedral. Stroll through the Lustgarten and on to Museumsinsel.

❸ Museumsinsel (see pp. 71–85) Select a few highlights at the museums on offer. Head west on Bodestrasse, then south on Oberwallstrasse to Französische Strasse.

❹ Gendarmenmarkt (see pp. 60–61) Visit the two churches on this handsome square. Exit on Kronenstrasse and walk west to Friedrichstrasse.

Bundestag
PLATZ DER REPUBLIK Reichstag
SCHEIDEMANNSTR REGIERUNG VIERTEL
Brandenburger Tor PARISER PLATZ
Brandenburger Tor
TIERGARTEN
Holocaust Monument
OLD REGIERUNG VIERTEL
VOSSSTRASSE
LENNÉSTR.
Sony Center LEIPZIGER PLATZ
KULTUR- FORUM POTSDAMER STR. **Potsdamer Platz** ❻ Potsdamer Platz
Daimler Contemporary Potsdamer Platz
MARLENE- DIETRICH- PLATZ Topograph des Terrc
LINKSTRASSE
KÖTHENER STR. STRESEMA
TILLA-DURIEUX-PARK
ASKANISCHER PLATZ
Mendelssohn- Bartholdy-Park
MENDELSSOHN- BARTHOLDY-PARK Anhal Bahnh
Möckernbrücke

**BERLIN IN A WEEKEND DAY 2 DISTANCE: 4.5 MILES (7.2 KM)
TIME: APPROX. 9 HOURS S-BAHN START: HACKESCHER MARKT**

LINIENSTRASSE

AUGUSTSTRASSE

Weinmeisterstrasse Ⓤ

FRIEDRICHSTRASSE

Oranienburger
Strasse

SCHEUNENVIERTEL

**Hackesche
Höfe** ❶

MONBIJOUPARK

Hackescher
Markt

Spree

Museumsinsel ⤳ Pergamonmuseum

MITTE

Ⓤ Friedrichstrasse

❸

Ⓤ Friedrichstrasse

Altes
Museum

❷ **Berliner
Dom**

Humboldt Forum

CHARLOTTENSTR.

UNTER DEN LINDEN

BEBEL-
PLATZ

Berliner
Schloss

WERDERSTR.

Spreekanal

Bunte SchokoWelt

❹ **Gendarmenmarkt**

GERTRAUDENSTR.

Ⓤ Hausvogteiplatz

KURSTR.

MOHRENSTRASSE

Ⓤ Stadtmitte
Mohrenstrasse

LEIPZIGER

STRASSE

Ⓤ Spittelmarkt

MAUERSTR.

KRAUSENSTRASSE

0   400 meters
0   400 yards

**Checkpoint
Charlie**

ZIMMERSTRASSE

WILHELMSTRASSE

Trabi
Museum

❺

KOCHSTRASSE

Ⓤ Kochstrasse

FRIEDRICHSTRASSE

Berlinische
Galerie

Jüdisches
Museum

...RASSE

Central Berlin
Area enlarged above

❻ **Potsdamer Platz** (see pp. 56–57) Round off
your day with a movie, cocktails, or dinner in
this state-of-the-art commercial quarter.

❺ **Checkpoint
Charlie** (see p. 57)
Examine all aspects
of Berlin as a divided city.
Walk west on Zimmerstrasse,
then Niederkirchnerstrasse, and
north on Stresemannstrasse.

Tips

This second day of your weekend tour covers the best of Berlin's cultural highlights. Follow the cross-references for detailed information on each. Use these tips for shortcuts when visiting on limited time. There are also suggestions for additional sights nearby and places to eat and drink along the way.

❶ **Hackesche Höfe** (see pp. 80–81)
There's always a buzz of anticipation and excitement as the courtyard cafés and boutiques wake to a new day. Stop for coffee at the ■ **HACKESCHER HOF RESTAURANT** *(Hof 1, open from 9 a.m.),* then treat yourself to a hip souvenir.

❷ **Berliner Dom** (see p. 75–76)
Before visiting Berlin's grand cathedral,

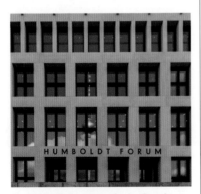

The Humboldt Forum stands, significantly, on Schlossplatz, or Castle Square.

take some time to explore the city's latest landmark, the ■ **HUMBOLDT FORUM** *(see pp. 76–77),* a brand-new culture and science hub run by four public institutions including Humboldt-Universität. The forum hosts museums, art installations, temporary exhibitions and events, as well as educational and research programs. Skip the detailed tour of the cathedral if you are short on time, but do climb to the top of its dome for one of the more intimate views of central Berlin. Before moving on, take a break in the pretty gardens—the ■ **LUSTGARTEN** (see p. 76)—opposite the cathedral's main entrance.

❸ **Museumsinsel** (see pp. 71–85)
Instead of trying to see all five museums in detail, pick one or two highlights from a couple— the Miletus and Ishtar Gates at the ■ **PERGAMONMUSEUM** (see pp. 74–75),

for example, or the ancient Greek statue known as the "Berlin Goddess" at the ■ **ALTES MUSEUM** (see p. 75). You'll make huge savings on ticket prices (and avoid waiting in line) if you buy one of several combined tickets available (see p. 175).

❹ Gendarmenmarkt (see pp. 60–61) This historic square is surrounded by shops and cafés. It is a great place to soak up the atmosphere of the city or to indulge in some retail therapy. Those with a sweet tooth can visit Ritter Sport's ■ **BUNTE SCHOKOWELT** (World of Chocolate; see p. 41), where you can make your own chocolate bars. Or stop in at the largest chocolatier in the world, ■ **RAUSCH SCHOKOLADENHAUS** (*Charlottenstrasse 60),* in the square's southwestern corner. In December, the square hosts one of Berlin's atmospheric ■ **CHRISTMAS MARKETS** (see pp. 120–121).

❺ Checkpoint Charlie (see p. 57) Take a detour past the ■ **TOPOGRAPHIE DES TERRORS** (*Niederkirchnerstrasse 8),* the former Gestapo headquarters. Close to Checkpoint Charlie, the ■ **TRABI MUSEUM** (see pp. 28–29) celebrates the state vehicle of the former GDR (DDR).

❻ Potsdamer Platz (see pp. 56–57) History buffs can inspect the remains of the ■ **BERLIN WALL** and the

CUSTOMIZING **YOUR DAY**

Instead of jostling with tourists at Checkpoint Charlie, seek out some retail therapy. Glamorous Friedrichstrasse exudes an alluring, NYC-style vibe, thanks to its mix of upscale offices, restaurants, and exclusive retail outlets. Department stores **Galeries Lafayette** *(Nos. 76–78)* and **Quartier 206** *(No. 71)* offer high-end design and fashion goods, while the enormous bookstore **Dussmann** *(No. 90)* has a very good English selection on the ground floor.

outdoor exhibitions explaining how the square was once a wasteland, while shopaholics will find great stores at the ■ **POTSDAMER PLATZ ARKADEN** (*Alte Potsdamer Strasse 7, potsdamerplatz. de).* For something cultural, head to the nearby ■ **KULTURFORUM** (see Neue Nationalgalerie and Bauhaus-Archiv; pp. 96–98) or drop in at ■ **DAIMLER CONTEMPORARY** (*Alte Potsdamer Strasse 5, art.daimler.com),* which hosts almost 2,000 works of art—mostly from the 20th century. For sustenance, ■ **WEILANDS** (*Eichhornstrasse 3, www. weilands-wellfood.de)* serves fresh, high-vitamin, low-calorie dishes in a bright and breezy canteen, while ■ **MOMMSENECK** (*Alte Potsdamer Strasse 1, www.mommseneck.de)* is the place to sample a range of international beers alongside traditional German dishes.

WHIRLWIND TOURS

Berlin for Fun

This east by west city tour combines skyline views and a Trabi Safari with some of the best classical music in Europe.

6 Berliner Philharmonie (see p. 29) Round off your day with a concert in one of Europe's finest music venues at the heart of Berlin's Kulturforum.

5 Deutsche Kinemathek (see p. 29) Explore Germany's fascinating cinematic history in this modern museum. Walk west on Potsdamer Strasse, then north on Scharounstrasse.

KAPELLE-UFE

SPREEBOGE PARK
Bundestag

PLATZ DER REPUBLIK

Haus der Kulturen der Welt

Reichstag

Spree

Brandenburg

SCHLOSSPARK BELLEVUE

Schloss Bellevue

Siegessäule

STRASSE DES 17. JUNI

TIERGARTEN

BELLEVUEALLEE

ALTONAER STRASSE

GROSSER STERNALLEE

BACHSTRASSE

STRASSE DES 17. JUNI

Tiergarten

Tiergarten 4

TIERGARTENUFER Neuer See

LICHTENSTEINALLEE

GROSSER WEG

TIERGARTENSTRASSE

Deutsche Kinemathek

6 5

Potsdame Plat.

Gemälde-galerie

Berliner Philharmonie

KULTURFORUM

Neue National-galerie

MARLENE-DIETRICH-PLATZ

DIPLOMATENVIERTEL

KLINGELHOFERSTR.

REICHPIETSCHUFER

SCHÖNEBERGER

TILLA-DURIEUX-PARK

LINKSTRASSE

KOTHENER

Mendelssohn Bartholdy-Pa

UFER

4 Tiergarten (see pp. 29, 98–99) Take a rowboat out on the Neuer See or climb the victory column in Berlin's sprawling park. Continue east on Tiergartenstrasse.

BERLIN FOR FUN DISTANCE: 6.2 MILES (10 KM)
TIME: 11–12 HOURS S-BAHN/U-BAHN START: ALEXANDERPLATZ

WHIRLWIND TOURS

❶ Fernsehturm (see pp. 28, 77–78) Ascend to the dizzy heights of this socialist TV tower for the best inner-city views of Berlin. Head north to Karl-Liebknecht-Strasse and follow Dircksenstrasse west to An der Spandauer Brücke. Take a right, and you'll soon hit Rosenthaler Strasse.

0   400 meters
0   400 yards

DOROTHEENSTÄDTISCHER FRIEDHOF
TORSTRASSE
LUISENSTRASSE
FRIEDRICHSTRASSE
AUGUSTSTRASSE
SCHEUNENVIERTEL
Weinmeisterstrasse
MÜNZSTRASSE
KARL-LIEBKNECHT-STR.
WADZECKSTR.
Oranienburger Strasse
Hackesche Höfe ❷
REINHARDTSTR.
MONBIJOUPARK
Hackescher Markt
ALEXANDER-PLATZ
Alexanderplatz
MITTE
Friedrichstrasse
Friedrichstrasse
Museumsinsel (Museum Island)
Berliner Dom
Fernsehturm ❶
REICHSTAGUFER
CHARLOTTENSTR.
UNTER DEN LINDEN
Deutsches Historisches Museum
NIKOLAIVIERTEL
REGIERUNGS-VIERTEL
ARISER PLATZ
BEBEL-PLATZ
PRINZESSINNEN-GARTEN
Brandenburger Tor
BEHRENSTR.
WERDERSTR.
Spree
FRANZÖSISCHE STR.
HOLOCAUST MONUMENT
GLINKASTR.
GENDARMENMARKT
Hausvogteiplatz
OLD REGIERUNGS-VIERTEL
Stadtmitte
Mohrenstrasse
LEIPZIGER STRASSE
Potsdamer Platz
Trabi Museum ❸
Checkpoint Charlie
Kochstrasse

Central Berlin
Area enlarged above

❷ Hackesche Höfe (see pp. 28, 80–81) Have a splurge on boutique treats. Return to Karl-Liebknecht-Strasse for bus 200 heading to Zoo at the intersection with Spandauer Strasse. Get off at Stadtmitte.

❸ Trabi Museum (see pp. 28–29) Indulge in a little *Ostalgie*, then hit the streets on a Trabi Safari. Take the U-Bahn (U6) to Friedrichstrasse, then the S-Bahn (S5 or S7) to Tiergarten.

Fernsehturm

1 Berlin's TV tower was once a major symbol of socialist East Germany. Today, its slim, tall form is present on everything from postcards to T-shirts. Take the elevator up to the space-age ball at the top for views of the city's major sights—the **Reichstag** (see pp. 62–63), **Brandenburger Tor** (see p. 54), and **Potsdamer Platz** (see pp. 56–57). You can even see the monumental **Olympiastadion** (see pp. 158–159) from here. Reservations are strongly recommended.

Panoramastrasse 1a • www.tv-turm.de • 030 24 75 75 875 • €€€€ • S-Bahn/ U-Bahn: Alexanderplatz

Hackesche Höfe

2 These eight lavishly restored courtyards have become one of central Berlin's most attractive shopping destinations. Originally opened in 1906 to house factories and offices, the courtyards now brim with boutiques and cultural venues. Scattered throughout are stores selling original clothing and footwear by independent designers. For souvenirs with a distinctly German twist, head to **Ampelmann** *(Hof 5, 030 44 72 64 38, www.ampelmann.de)* for an incredible range of goods related to the famed East German traffic-light man.

Rosenthaler Strasse 40–41 • www.hackesche-hoefe.de • S-Bahn: Hackescher Markt

Join other Trabant enthusiasts on the Trabi Museum's fun safari.

Trabi Museum

3 This enterprise pays homage to the "Volkswagen of the East" in an exhibition that combines a straight history of the Trabant with a little *Ostalgie*—a play on the German words for East *(Ost)* and nostalgia *(Nostalgie)*. In the former GDR (DDR), years used to pass between ordering a Trabant and actually taking delivery. Today, you can get behind the wheel of a Trabant yourself and join a Trabi Safari (*from €59*) through the streets of Berlin (driver's license required). You'll have to book in advance (see *www.trabi-safari.de* for details).

Zimmerstrasse 14–15 • www.trabi-museum.com • 030 30 20 10 30 • €
• U-Bahn: Kochstrasse

Tiergarten

4 If you're visiting the park at dusk, a magical sight awaits you at the **Gaslaternen-Freilichtmuseum** (Gas Lantern Museum; *Joseph-Haydn-Strasse, 030 90 25 41 24*), whose outdoor exhibition displays 90 historic gas lanterns from Berlin and other European cities. Beautifully restored, they illuminate a winding path from dusk. If visiting in summer, head to **Neuer See** for a row on the lake. Both the museum and the lake are close to Tiergarten S-Bahn station.

Strasse des 17. Juni • S-Bahn: Tiergarten

Deutsche Kinemathek

5 The entertaining and modern multimedia Film and Television Museum is a must for cinema buffs. Spanning Germany's entire filmmaking history, there are posters and photos, film costumes, scripts, and original props. Watch for dedicated sections on stars such as Marlene Dietrich and *Metropolis* director Fritz Lang.

Potsdamer Strasse 2 • www.deutsche-kinemathek.de • 030 30 09 030 • €€€
• Closed Tues. • S-Bahn/U-Bahn: Potsdamer Platz

Berliner Philharmonie

6 Book tickets in advance for Berlin's Philharmonic Orchestra, either in the **Grosser Saal** (Great Hall) or the **Kammermusiksaal** (Chamber Music Hall). If visiting between August and September, check out the program for the **Musikfest Berlin** (*www.berlinerfestspiele.de*).

Herbert-von-Karajan-Strasse 1 • www.berliner-philharmoniker.de • 030 25 48 80
• €€–€€€€€ • S-Bahn/U-Bahn: Potsdamer Platz

Berlin for Spies

Follow this spy trail through Berlin's totalitarian east—the hub of European espionage during the Cold War years.

❷ **Berliner Unterwelten** (see p. 32)
Explore the dark and secret past of underground Berlin. Take the S-Bahn (S8) to Landsberger Allee. Change here for a tram (M5) heading to Zingster Strasse and get off at Liebenwalder Strasse. Walk southeast to Genslerstrasse.

❶ **Gedenkstätte Berliner Mauer** (see pp. 32, 130–131)
Trace the path of the Berlin Wall to gain an understanding of the role it played in dividing the city during the Cold War years. Walk north on Brunnenstrasse.

WHIRLWIND TOURS

BERLIN FOR SPIES DISTANCE: 15 MILES (24 KM) TIME: 9 HOURS S-BAHN START: NORDBAHNHOF

❸ Gedenkstätte Hohenschönhausen (see p. 32)
Hear stories from past inmates at this former Stasi prison. Return to Liebenwalder Strasse. Catch a bus (256) south to Frankfurter Allee and walk west.

❹ Stasi-Museum (see p. 33)
Take a tour of House 1—the former headquarters of the Ministry of State Security. Take the U-Bahn (U5) from Magdalenenstrasse to Alexanderplatz and cross the square.

❺ DDR Museum
(see p. 33) Experience life as it was for civilians under the former Soviet regime.

East Berlin
Area enlarged above

IN **THE KNOW**

Opposite the Visitor Center at the Gedenkstätte Berliner Mauer stands **Nordbahnhof station,** home to an exhibition on the Ghost Stations of the GDR (DDR) years. These stations were closed during the division, despite being on functioning East–West lines, because they represented a risk of escape. Stop by to read stories of would-be escapees who fell prey to Stasi booby traps and tales of the few who succeeded in fleeing.

Gedenkstätte Berliner Mauer

1 The Berlin Wall Memorial stretches the length of Bernauer Strasse. Drop into the **Visitor Center** for exhibitions relating to the memorial. Listen to recorded accounts at each stage and discover the fates of those who tried to escape here. Ascend to a platform that overlooks a stretch of the Death Strip as it was when manned by guards in watchtowers.

Bernauer Strasse 111 and 119 • www.berliner-mauer -gedenkstaette.de • 030 21 30 85 123 • Visitor Center closed Mon. • S-Bahn: Nordbahnhof

Berliner Unterwelten

2 Walk beneath the city streets with Berlin Underworlds, an organization operating a range of exploratory tours from a bunker at Gesundbrunnen S-Bahn station. Tour 1 *(times and days often vary by season)* explores one of the few remaining underground bunkers, as it was left after World War II. Check the website for tour requirements ahead of your trip.

Brunnenstrasse 105 • www.berliner-unterwelten.de • 030 49 91 05 17 • €€€ • Info Center closed Tues. • S-Bahn: Gesundbrunnen

Gedenkstätte Hohenschönhausen

3 With interiors that remain much as they were when this sinister institution was in its heyday, the Hohenschönhausen Memorial offers insight into prison life under the Soviet regime. The exhibition is free of charge, but it is worth indulging in a guided tour, often led by former inmates. If you don't speak German, tours in English are also available *(daily at 10:40 a.m., 12:40 p.m., and 2:40 p.m.; check in advance for changes)*.

Genslerstrasse 66 • www.stiftung-hsh.de • 030 98 60 82 30 • €€ • Closed Jan. 1, Dec. 24–26 and 31 • Tram: M5 (Freienwalder Strasse)

Stasi-Museum

4 Housed in the former headquarters of the Ministry of State Security, this museum relates the chilling story of how one half of the population spied on the other. Seek out the intriguing displays of the gadgetry that underpinned their surveillance activities.

Normannenstrasse 20, Haus 1 • www.stasimuseum.de • 030 55 36 854 • €€
• Closed Jan. 1, Dec. 24–31 • U-Bahn: Magdalenenstrasse

DDR Museum

5 Discover the truth about life for ordinary civilians, breathe in the original aroma of an East German living room, and pick up the phone (which you'll find has been bugged). If you think you're tough enough, take on the challenge of a Stasi interrogation.

Karl-Liebknecht-Strasse 1 • www.ddr-museum.de • 030 84 71 23 730 • €€€
• S-Bahn: Hackescher Markt

Look closely to see doors hidden in this photographic wall. They open to reveal Stasi secrets.

WHIRLWIND **TOUR**

❹ DZ Bank Building
(see p. 37) Marvel at Frank Gehry's remarkable atrium with its split-level spaces, curving glass ceilings, and extraordinary conference room. Walk north on Ebertstrasse.

❺ Reichstag (see pp. 37, 62–63)
Admire Sir Norman Foster's huge glass dome, one of the most symbolic structures of the post-wall era. Walk east on Scheidemannstrasse, then north on Heinrich-von-Gagern-Strasse.

❻ Bundeskanzleramt (see p. 37) Abstract and oversized or a welcome emblem of modern democracy? See what you make of the German chancellor's new living and working space. Take the U-Bahn (U5) from Bundestag to Alexanderplatz, then at the intersection with Grunerstrasse take bus 248 for four stops.

❼ Jüdisches Museum (see pp. 37, 148–149)
Contemplate Daniel Libeskind's skill in interpreting the complex story of Jewish-German relations through his innovative architecture—both inside and out.

WHIRLWIND TOURS

**BERLIN FOR CONTEMPORARY ARCHITECTURE FANS DISTANCE: 5 MILES (8 KM)
TIME: 8 HOURS S-BAHN START: HACKESCHER MARKT**

Berlin for Contemporary Architecture Fans

See how the crème de la crème of contemporary architects has changed the face of Berlin since the fall of the Berlin Wall.

❶ Neues Museum (see pp. 36, 82–85) Discover why people waited in line for six hours to see the internal restoration of this museum *before* it was filled with exhibits. Walk through Lustgarten and cross the Spree River onto Unter den Linden.

❸ Akademie der Künste (see p. 36) Step beyond the glass facade at the Academy of Arts to discover an interior by Günter Behnisch with a spectacularly expressionistic twist. Head next door.

❷ Deutsches Historisches Museum (see pp. 36, 59) Consider I. M. Pei's success in rising to the challenge of designing a contemporary annex for the most prominent baroque building on Unter den Linden.
Continue west to Pariser Platz.

Central Berlin
Area enlarged above

Neues Museum

1 David Chipperfield's sophisticated 2005 restoration of the New Museum makes no attempt to hide the extensive damage sustained during World War II. You'll see intricately restored murals and bullet-strafed walls juxtaposed with assertive new spaces and solid oak doors that could pass as part of the original building. Its new fitting entrance is at the **James-Simon-Galerie**, a grand colonnade that serves as a service center for all of the museums on the island.

James-Simon-Galerie, Bodestrasse 1–3 • www.smb.museum • 030 26 64 24 242 • €€€ • Dec. 24 • U-Bahn: Museumsinsel

Deutsches Historisches Museum

2 I. M. Pei's sleek glass-and-limestone extension of the German Historical Museum contrasts strongly with the heavily decorated baroque Zeughaus (armory) next door. Yet see how it defers to the older building through the transparency of its vast glazed atrium lobby.

Unter den Linden 2 • www.dhm.de • 030 20304 750 • €€ (temporary exhibitions) • Closed Dec. 24 • S-Bahn/U-Bahn: Friedrichstrasse

Akademie der Künste

3 What little survived World War II is now encased in a transparent structure of cascading steel-and-glass components that somehow contain an archive, an auditorium, offices, a café, and a reception room. As you consider this remarkable interior, you'll appreciate that it is no mean feat of structural engineering.

Pariser Platz 4 • www.adk.de • 030 20 05 71 000 • €€ (temporary exhibitions) • S-Bahn/U-Bahn: Brandenburger Tor

Curving glass ceilings separate the floors of DZ Bank's complex, multistoried foyer.

DZ Bank Building

4 Frank Gehry's sober sandstone-and-glass facade hides the organic exuberance of his interior, which features an enormous horse-head-shaped, zinc-clad conference room and a steel-and-glass floor.

Pariser Platz 3 • www.axica.de • 030 20 00 860 • S-Bahn/U-Bahn: Brandenburger Tor

Reichstag

5 Norman Foster's 1999 renovation of the originally neoclassical national parliamentary building is punctuated with accents of war damage and Russian graffiti and crowned by the much talked about glass dome. The high-tech design is also superefficient, fueled by vegetable oil, geothermal energy, and the sun.

Platz der Republik 1 • www.bundestag.de • 030 22 73 21 52 • Closed Dec. 24.
• S-Bahn/U-Bahn: Brandenburger Tor

Bundeskanzleramt

6 Inspired by such disparate works as the mosques of Isfahan and the buildings of American architect Louis Kahn, the Chancellery is a focal point of a much larger scheme designed by Axel Schultes and Charlotte Frank. They created what they call a "Federal Ribbon"—a corridor of government buildings that crosses the Spree River twice at former Cold War boundaries, thereby symbolically reconnecting the city.

Willy-Brandt-Strasse 1 • 0180 27 20 000 • U-Bahn: Bundestag

Jüdisches Museum

7 A crucial contribution to Jewish-German reconciliation in the wake of the horrors of the 20th century, Daniel Libeskind's lightning-bolt floorplan combines with slashed windows, zinc cladding, concrete voids, and symbol-laden landscapes to create one of the most radical buildings in Europe today.

Lindenstrasse 9–14 • www.jmberlin.de • 030 25 99 33 00 • €€ (temporary exhibitions)
• Closed Rosh Hashanah, Yom Kippur, Nov. 12, and Dec. 24 • U-Bahn: Kochstrasse

Berlin in a Weekend with Kids

*A fun-packed day with sea creatures to stroke, buttons to push,
and chocolate—not only to eat, but to make as well.*

❶ Sea Life (see p. 40) Visit
the AquaDom in this exciting
underwater world. Walk south on
Spandauer Strasse, then west on
Karl-Liebknecht-Strasse.

❷ DDR Museum (see p. 40) Enjoy
some push-button fun at one of the
city's most interactive museums. Return
to Karl-Liebknecht-Strasse and proceed
east along it.

❸ Little Big City (see p. 40) Sightsee this
miniature city within the city. Exit and walk
a few steps south to reach the space-age
Fernsehturm.

**BERLIN WITH KIDS, DAY 1 DISTANCE: 3 MILES (5 KM)
TIME: 7 HOURS S-BAHN START: HACKESCHER MARKT**

❹ Fernsehturm (see pp. 41, 77–78) Take in the spectacular views from Berlin's tallest building. Hop on the S-Bahn (S5) at Alexanderplatz and get off at Unter den Linden.

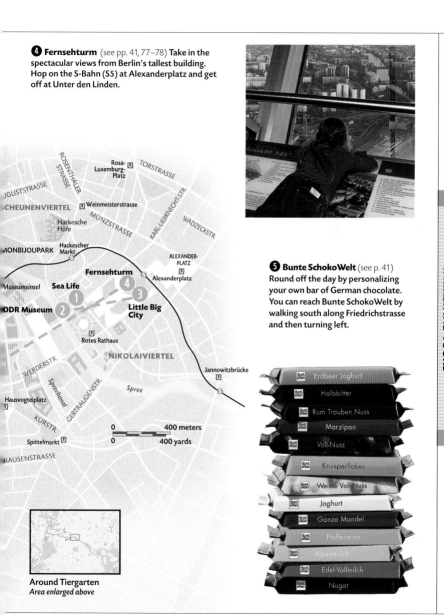

❺ Bunte SchokoWelt (see p. 41) Round off the day by personalizing your own bar of German chocolate. You can reach Bunte SchokoWelt by walking south along Friedrichstrasse and then turning left.

ROSENTHALER STRASSE
Rosa-Luxemburg-Platz
TORSTRASSE
AUGUSTSTRASSE
SCHEUNENVIERTEL
Weinmeisterstrasse
KARL-LIEBKNECHT-STR.
WADZECKSTR.
Hackesche Höfe
MÜNZSTRASSE
MONBIJOUPARK
Hackescher Markt
ALEXANDER-PLATZ
Fernsehturm
Alexanderplatz
Museumsinsel
Sea Life
DDR Museum
Little Big City
Rotes Rathaus
NIKOLAIVIERTEL
WERDERSTR.
Spreekanal
GERTRAUDENSTR.
Spree
Jannowitzbrücke
Hausvogteiplatz
KURSTR.
Spittelmarkt
0   400 meters
0   400 yards
RAUSENSTRASSE

Around Tiergarten
Area enlarged above

Erdbeer Joghurt
Halbbitter
Rum Trauben Nuss
Marzipan
Voll-Nuss
Knusperflakes
Weisse Voll-Nuss
Joghurt
Ganze Mandel
Pfefferminz
Alpenmilch
Edel-Vollmilch
Nugat

Sea Life

1 Indulge your kids in some fishy fun in this vibrant underwater world. Head straight for the **Interactive Rockpool,** with its sea stars, crabs, and sea anemones, some of which may be touched. The real highlight comes in the shape of the 80-foot-tall (24 m) **AquaDom**—the largest cylindrical fish tank in the world—complete with a coral reef and 100 species of beautiful, exotic fish that include triggerfish, blowfish, and silver moonfish. Due to limited admission capacities, entry is only guaranteed with an online reservation.

Spandauer Strasse 3 • www.visitsealife.com • 01806 66 69 0101 • €€€€ • Closed Dec. 24 • U-Bahn: Rotes Rathaus

SAVVY **TRAVELER**

Check the Sea Life website in advance to see if you can plan your visit to coincide with one of the many daily feeding times.

DDR Museum

2 Step into the former German Democratic Republic at this fun hands-on museum. Kids can sit behind the wheel of a Trabant, the iconic East German car—they can even turn on the ignition. See what's cooking in the authentic East Berlin kitchen and watch the kids play at being spies with hidden Stasi microphones. There are endless drawers and doors to open throughout, each one providing a new insight into this very different world.

Karl-Liebknecht-Strasse 1 • www.ddr-museum.de • 030 84 71 23 730 • €€€ • S-Bahn: Hackescher Markt

Little Big City

3 Highly interactive, fun, colorful, and educational. What more could you ask? In this "Little Big Berlin" not only is the city reconstructed, but also 750 years of its history. Have fun trying to name the 100 recreated buildings and appreciate the vibrant models boasting more than 6,000 little citizens. Games, holograms, and interactive installations also help bring the city to life.

Panoramastrasse 1a • www.officiallittlebigcity.com • 01806 25 7106 • €€€€ • S-Bahn/U-Bahn: Alexanderplatz

Fernsehturm

4 Berlin's rocket-shaped TV Tower is a major draw for kids. Not only does a high-speed elevator whisk them up 650 feet (200 m) in just 40 seconds, but there's a rotating restaurant at the top (the **Sphere;** *030 24 75 75 875, €€–€€€*). Purchase a ticket online ahead of your trip, and you can reserve a specific time to visit.

Panoramastrasse 1a • www.tv-turm.de • 030 24 75 75 875 • €€€€
• S-Bahn/U-Bahn: Alexanderplatz

Bunte SchokoWelt

5 Ritter Sport's colorful flagship store features a **History and Making of Chocolate** exhibit where kids can learn all about Germany's best known chocolate brand. There is also a café serving to-die-for hot chocolate. Best of all, kids can design their own candy bars and watch them being made (*€€€*). Book in advance.

Französische Strasse 24 • www.ritter-sport.de • 030 20 09 50 80
• U-Bahn: Unter den Linden

Kids have everything on hand for making Ritter Sport chocolate bars of their own.

Berlin in a Weekend with Kids

Today's tour is one big adventure that sees kids playing with animals, gadgets, and gizmos.

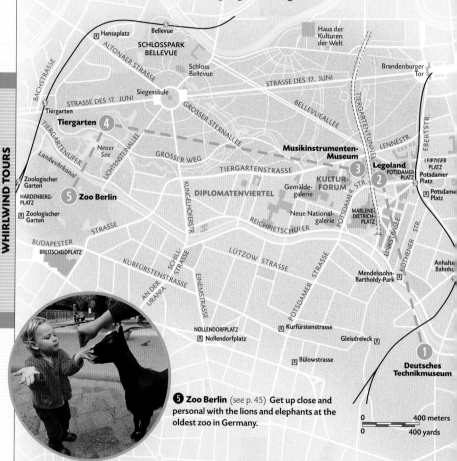

WHIRLWIND TOURS

Hansaplatz
Bellevue
SCHLOSSPARK BELLEVUE
Haus der Kulturen der Welt
ALTONAER STRASSE
Schloss Bellevue
Brandenburger Tor
BACHSTRASSE
STRASSE DES 17. JUNI
Siegessäule
STRASSE DES 17. JUNI
Tiergarten
Tiergarten **4**
GROSSER STERNALLEE
BELLEVUEALLEE
TIERGARTENTUNNEL
LENNESTR.
EBERTSTR.
TIERGARTENUFER
Neuer See
LICHTENSTEINALLEE
GROSSER WEG
TIERGARTENSTRASSE
Musikinstrumenten-**Museum**
3 Legoland
POTSDAMER PLATZ
I FIPZIGFR PLATZ
Potsdamer Platz
Landwehrkanal
Zoologischer Garten
HARDENBERG-PLATZ
Zoo Berlin **5**
DIPLOMATENVIERTEL
KLINGELHÖFERSTR.
Gemälde-galerie
KULTUR-FORUM
POTSDAMER STR.
2
MARLENE-DIETRICH-PLATZ
Potsdame Platz
Zoologischer Garten
Neue National-galerie
REICHPIETSCHUFER
LINKSTRASSE
KÖTHENER STR.
BUDAPESTER
STRASSE
BREITSCHEIDPLATZ
KURFÜRSTENSTRASSE
SCHILL STRASSE
LÜTZOW STRASSE
POTSDAMER STRASSE
Mendelssohn-Bartholdy-Park
Anhalte Bahnhc
AN DER URANIA
EINEMSTRASSE
NOLLENDORFPLATZ
Nollendorfplatz
Kurfürstenstrasse
Gleisdreieck
Bülowstrasse
1
Deutsches Technikmuseum

5 Zoo Berlin (see p. 45) Get up close and personal with the lions and elephants at the oldest zoo in Germany.

| 0 | 400 meters |
| 0 | 400 yards |

BERLIN WITH KIDS, DAY 2 DISTANCE: 3.75 MILES (5.5 KM) TIME: 7 HOURS U-BAHN START: MÖCKERNBRÜCKE

❶ Deutsches Technikmuseum (see p. 44) Watch your kids have fun coming to grips with technology. Head north; cross the Landwehrkanal by the pedestrian bridge, then Elise-Tilse Park. From Anhalter Bahnhof take the S-Bahn (S2) to Potsdamer Platz.

❷ Legoland (see p. 44–45) You'll see the giant Lego giraffe as you approach this mini-brick haven. Turn right onto Potsdamer Platz and then take Ben-Gurion-Strasse on the right.

❸ Musikinstrumenten-Museum (see p. 45) Hundreds of musical instruments await you to learn while having fun. Start again from Ben-Gurion-Strasse and keep walking until you get deeper into the park.

❹ Tiergarten (see pp. 45, 98–99) Enjoy the myriad pleasures and playgrounds of Berlin's royal park. Wend your way to the park's southwest corner and on to Hardenbergplatz.

Around Tiergarten
Area enlarged above

WHIRLWIND TOURS

Deutsches Technikmuseum

1 Extensive coverage of all things technological awaits the curious child at the German Museum of Technology. Instead of trying to see everything, focus on just one or two of the 19 permanent exhibitions on offer, from transportation and computer science to paper technology and textile work. Kids can learn how just about everything gets made—from medicines to suitcases—and there are interactive exhibits throughout.

Trebbiner Strasse 9 • technikmuseum.berlin • 030 9025 40 • €€ • Closed Mon.
• U-Bahn: Möckernbrücke

Legoland

2 Enter the realm of one of the world's best-selling toys, which has sparked the imaginations of millions. Legoland will guide you through pools overflowing with colorful bricks, roller

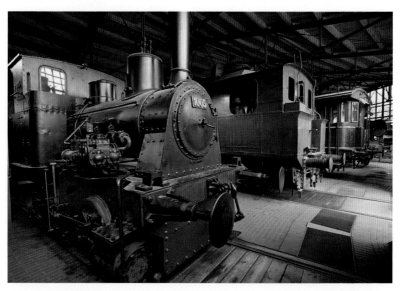

Life-size planes, trains, ships, and lots, lots more at the German Museum of Technology

coasters and even a factory where the famous bricks are made from plastic.

Potsdamer Strasse 4 • legolanddiscoverycentre.com/berlin • €€€€€ • S-Bahn/U-Bahn: Potsdamer Platz

Musikinstrumenten-Museum

3 The Museum of Musical Instruments boasts about 800 pieces (of the more than 3,600 owned) and offers a playful visitor experience: Some open cases contain mechanisms or real instruments to play (try the theremin!). On Saturdays at noon, don't miss the concert of the colossal Wurlitzer organ, a special keyboard instrument built to soundtrack silent films and which also reproduces the chirping of birds.

Ben-Gurion-Strasse • simpk.de • 030 25 48 11 78 • €€ • Closed Mon. • S-Bahn/U-Bahn: Potsdamer Platz

Tiergarten

4 Berlin's largest park has endless opportunities for kids: playgrounds, forested areas, lakes, and meadows. The largest play area is on John-Foster-Dulles-Allee and features a sandbox, tire swings, and a climbing net. It's a good 20-minute walk from the S-Bahn station, but well worth it—take a picnic for sustenance.

Strasse des 17. Juni • S-Bahn: Tiergarten

Zoo Berlin

5 The oldest (1844) animal park in Germany boasts 1,200 species—more than any other zoo in Europe. Plan your trip to coincide with feeding time for the monkeys (*1:30 p.m.*)— it's a riotous affair.

Hardenbergplatz 8 • www.zoo-berlin.de • 030 25 40 10 • €€€€ • S-Bahn/ U-Bahn: Zoologischer Garten

GOOD **EATS**

■ **ANDY'S DINER & BAR**
Overlooking Sea Life's AquaDom, this American-style diner serves star-studded classics from pork ribs to burgers. **Karl-Liebknecht-Strasse 5, 030 97 89 41 20, €€**

■ **THE DAWG**
Next to the zoo, this trendy eatery specializes in hot dogs. There's something for everyone, even an octopus dog! It offers seating in a spacious outdoor area, while inside huge windows provide views of the baboon garden. **Budapester Strasse 38-50, 030 89 06 42 10, €€**

WHIRLWIND TOURS

PART 2

Berlin's Neighborhoods

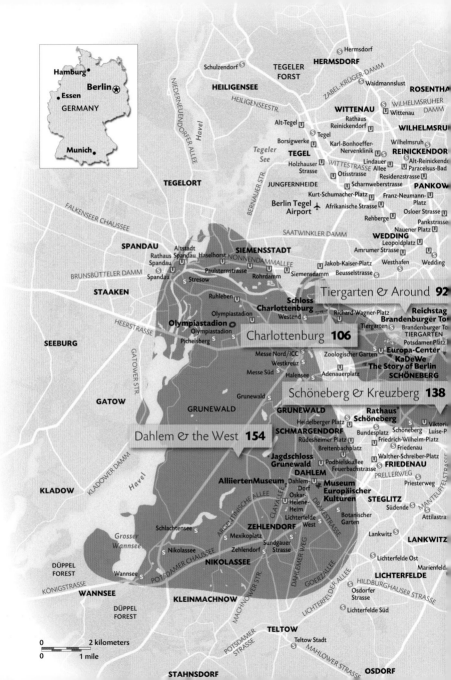

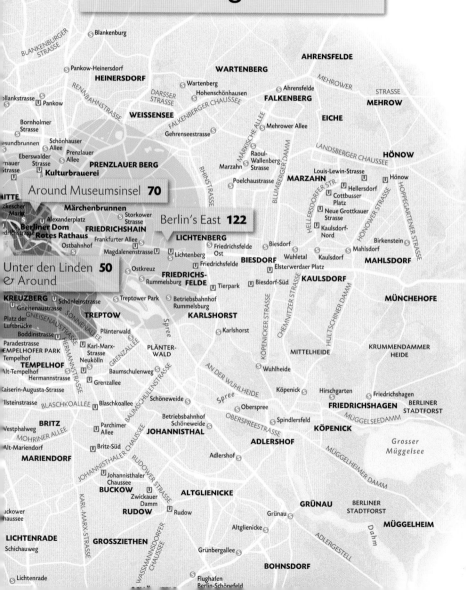

Berlin's Neighborhoods

Blankenburg

BLANKENBURGER STRASSE

Pankow-Heinersdorf
HEINERSDORF

WARTENBERG

AHRENSFELDE

ollankstrasse
Pankow

DARSSER STRASSE

Wartenberg

Hohenschönhausen

MEHROWER STRASSE

RENNBAHNSTRASSE

Ahrensfelde
FALKENBERG

MEHROW

FALKENBERGER CHAUSSEE

WEISSENSEE

EICHE

Mehrower Allee

Bornholmer Strasse

Gehrenseestrasse

esundbrunnen
Allee

Schönhauser Allee

MÄRKISCHE ALLEE

Eberswalder Strasse

Prenzlauer Allee

Raoul-Wallenberg-Strasse

Marzahn

LANDSBERGER CHAUSSEE

HÖNOW

nauer Strasse

PRENZLAUER BERG

Kulturbrauerei

RHINSTRASSE

Poelchaustrasse

Louis-Lewin-Strasse
MARZAHN

Hönow

Around Museuminsel **70**

BLUMBERGER DAMM

Hellersdorf

ITTE

ckescher
Markt

Märchenbrunnen

Storkower Strasse

Berlin's East **122**

Cottbusser Platz

HÖNOWER STRASSE

Alexanderplatz

Berliner Dom
Rotes Rathaus

FRIEDRICHSHAIN

Neue Grottkauer Strasse

drichstrasse

Frankfurter Allee

LICHTENBERG

Kaulsdorf-Nord

HELLERSDORFER STR.

HOPPEGARTENER STRASSE

Ostbahnhof

Magdalenenstrasse

Friedrichsfelde

Biesdorf

Birkenstein

Lichtenberg
Ost

Unter den Linden **50**
& Around

Ostkreuz

Friedrichsfelde

BIESDORF

Wuhletal

Kaulsdorf

Mahlsdorf

MAHLSDORF

Elsterwerdaer Platz

FRIEDRICHS-
Rummelsburg
FELDE

Tierpark

Biesdorf-Süd

KAULSDORF

KREUZBERG

Schöneinstrasse

Treptower Park

Betriebsbahnhof
Rummelsburg

CHEMNITZER STRASSE

MÜNCHEHOFE

Gneisenaustrasse

TREPTOW

KARLSHORST

Platz der
Luftbrücke

GNEISENAUSTRASSE

SONNENALLEE

Boddinstrasse

Plänterwald

Karlshorst

HULTSCHINER DAMM

Paradestrasse

MPELHOFER PARK
TEMPELHOF

Karl-Marx-
Strasse
Neukölln

GRENZALLEE

PLÄNTER-
WALD

KÖPENICKER STRASSE

MITTELHEIDE

KRUMMENDAMMER
HEIDE

Alt-Tempelhof

Hermannstrasse

Baumschulenweg

AN DER WUHLHEIDE

Wuhlheide

Kaiserin-Augusta-Strasse

Grenzallee

BLASCHKOALLEE

Blaschkoallee

Schöneweide

Spree

Köpenick

Hirschgarten

Friedrichshagen

llsteinstrasse

Oberspree

FRIEDRICHSHAGEN

BERLINER
STADTFORST

BRITZ

Parchimer
Allee

Betriebsbahnhof
Schöneweide

OBERSPREESTRASSE

Spindlersfeld

MÜGGELSEEDAMM

Vestphalweg

JOHANNISTHAL

KÖPENICK

MOHRINER ALLEE

Britz-Süd

BAUMSCHULENSTRASSE

Alt-Mariendorf

ADLERSHOF

Grosser
Müggelsee

MARIENDORF

RUDOWER STRASSE

Adlershof

MÜGGELHEIMER DAMM

JOHANNISTHALER CHAUSSEE

Johannisthaler
Chaussee
BUCKOW

ALTGLIENICKE

GRÜNAU

BERLINER
STADTFORST

Zwickauer
Damm
RUDOW

Rudow

Grünau

MÜGGELHEIM

uckower
haussee

KARL-MARX-STRASSE

Altglienicke

ADLERGESTELL

Dahme

LICHTENRADE

GROSSZIETHEN

Grünbergallee

WASSMANNSDORFER CHAUSSEE

Schichauweg

BOHNSDORF

Lichtenrade

Flughafen
Berlin-Schönefeld

Unter den Linden & Around

Stroll the streets of this neighborhood and it is difficult to imagine that, during the Cold War years, the Brandenburger Tor (Brandenburg Gate) was stranded in wasteland with a near-derelict Reichstag close by. Stopping just short of the Berlin Wall, the city's historic boulevard, Unter den Linden, became all but redundant for almost 30 years. Today, however, these landmarks define a neighborhood that is every bit the epicenter of a vital European capital city—just as it was in the days of the Prussian Empire. While Unter den Linden and Gendarmenmarkt hark back to the 18th and 19th centuries, Checkpoint Charlie, Bebelplatz, and the Holocaust Monument are poignant reminders of a more recent past. And all the while, the soaring skyscrapers at Potsdamer Platz shimmer with a dynamism that screams future.

◀ **The design for the Brandenburg Gate, Berlin's most famous monument, took inspiration from the entrance to the Acropolis in Athens.**

Unter den Linden & Around

From Prussian grandeur to Cold War nostalgia, the monuments
of Berlin's historic center reveal the city's vibrant past.

❶ Reichstag (see pp. 62–63) Start with breakfast at the Reichstag. Make your way to Scheidemannstrasse. Head east until you reach Ebertstrasse, where the Brandenburg Gate will come into view. Approach Pariser Platz from here.

❷ Pariser Platz (see p. 54) **Enter** this spacious square through the mighty Brandenburg Gate. On leaving, return to Ebertstrasse and walk south.

❸ Holocaust Monument (see p. 55) Contemplate the fate of many Jews during the Nazi era at this sobering monument. Continue south on Ebertstrasse.

❹ Potsdamer Platz (see pp. 56–57) **Marvel** at the ultramodern buildings of this once-derelict square. Walk south on Stresemannstrasse, then turn onto Niederkirchnerstrasse, heading east.

Map labels:
Spree
REICHSTAGSUFER
PLATZ DER REPUBLIK
❶ Reichstag
WILHELMSTRASSE
DOROTHEEN
REGIERUNGS VIERTEL
Brandenburger Tor
STRASSE DES 17. JUNI
❷ Pariser Platz
UNTER DE
Brandenburger Tor
TIERGARTEN
Holocaust Monument ❸
CORA-BERLINER-STRASSE
TIERGARTENTUNNEL
LENNESTRASSE
BELLEVUESTR.
EBERTSTRASSE
Mohrenstrasse
VOSSSTRASSE
LEIPZIGER PLATZ
Bahntower
Potsdamer Platz ❹
LEIPZIGER
POTSDAMER STR.
Potsdamer Platz
Potsdamer Platz
MARLENE-DIETRICH-PLATZ
Quartier Potsdamer Platz
NIEDERKIRCHNERSTR
LINKSTRASSE
TILLA-DURIEUX-PARK
KÖTHENER STRASSE
STRESEMANNSTRASSE
ANHALT

UNTER DEN LINDEN & AROUND   DISTANCE: 3.5 MILES (5.6 KM)
TIME: APPROX. 10 HOURS   S-BAHN/U-BAHN START: BRANDENBURGER TOR

⑩ Gendarmenmarkt (see pp. 60–61) Wind up at lively Gendarmenmarkt, with its two 18th-century churches and striking concert hall.

⑨ Bebelplatz (see p. 60) Seek out the low-key memorial at the center of this sedate square. From the south side of it turn right and take Markgrafenstrasse.

⑧ Neue Wache (see p. 59) Drop in to see Käthe Kollwitz's stirring sculpture, then cross Unter den Linden.

❼ Deutsches Historisches Museum (see p. 59) Select highlights from the 2,000 years of history on offer. Return to Unter den Linden and turn right; the next stop is just a few steps ahead.

❻ PalaisPopulaire (see p. 58) Plunge into contemporary art and culture within the walls of a noble mansion for Prussian princesses. Cross Unter den Linden.

❺ Checkpoint Charlie (see p. 57) Follow the former wall trail along Niederkirchnerstrasse to Checkpoint Charlie and the Wall Museum. Walk north on Friedrichstrasse, take Leipziger Strasse to the right, then Jerusalemer Strasse to the left and north again to Unter den Linden.

The terrace café at Hotel Adlon on Pariser Platz is a major draw for tourists hoping to spot the odd celebrity.

Reichstag

1 See pp. 62–63.

Platz der Republik 1 • www.bundestag.de
• 030 22 73 21 52 • Closed Dec. 24
• S-Bahn/U-Bahn: Brandenburger Tor

Pariser Platz

2 Approaching Pariser Platz from the west, you'll pass straight through the monumental **Brandenburger Tor** (Brandenburg Gate). This gate symbolizes victory, peace, division, and unity all in one. Admire the sextet of Doric columns topped with the Quadriga, or Goddess of Victory, before strolling through the gate and into Pariser Platz. The meticulously restored buildings that flank this elegant square include the British, French, and U.S. embassies. For art lovers, **Max Liebermann Haus** (*No. 7, www.stiftungbrandenburgertor.de, 030 22 63 30 16, closed Mon.–Wed.*), the former home of the German Impressionist painter, hosts rotating art exhibitions organized by the Brandenburg Gate Foundation. Established in 1696, the glass-fronted **Akademie der Künste** (Academy of Arts; see p. 36) hosts exhibitions across a number of disciplines, including photography, fine art, and architecture. To escape the crowds for a moment, head to the **Room of Silence** (*www.raum-der-stille-im-brandenburger-tor.de*) on the north side of the Brandenburg Gate, built specifically for visitors to rest and reflect on the city's troubled history.

Pariser Platz • S-Bahn/U-Bahn: Brandenburger Tor

UNTER DEN LINDEN & AROUND

Holocaust Monument

3 Some 2,700 concrete slabs occupy Peter Eisenman's enormous **Stelenfeld** (Field of Staele) at the **Denkmal für die ermordeten Juden Europas** (Monument for the Murdered Jews of Europe). The slabs—unmistakable in their association with sarcophagi—differ in height and sit in neat rows on an undulating floor. Walk directly off the street and among the stelae, following the narrow paths as they dip and rise. An **Ort der Information** (Information Center; *closed Mon., Jan. 1, and Dec. 24–26*) beneath the monument pays personal tribute to the Jewish victims of the Holocaust. You'll see their names projected onto walls and can watch more than 150 video interviews with survivors (in English translation). Across the road on Ebertstrasse, the **Denkmal für die im Nationalsozialismus verfolgten Homosexuellen** (Memorial to Homosexuals Persecuted under Nazism) consists of a concrete cube showing alternating looped films of gay couples kissing.

Cora-Berliner-Strasse 1 • www.stiftung-denkmal.de • 030 26 39 430
• S-Bahn/U-Bahn: Brandenburger Tor

The Holocaust Monument is intended to provoke feelings of disorientation and unease.

A mini-world in itself, the vast, eco-friendly Sony Center on Potsdamer Platz contains conference rooms, museums, clubs, restaurants, offices, apartments, and stores.

Potsdamer Platz

4 Celebrated as one of Europe's most vibrant squares during the 1920s, what was left of Potsdamer Platz after the Allied bombings of World War II was leveled to make way for the Berlin Wall in 1961. After the fall of the wall, major investors including Daimler-Benz AG and Sony commissioned a team of internationally renowned architects led by Renzo Piano and Christoph Kohlbecker to catapult the square into the 21st century. What you see today is a dynamic commercial space that is distinguished by its soaring modernist skyscrapers. The glass-and-chrome offices of **Deutsche Bahn** (*No. 2*) and the art deco **Ritz-Carlton Hotel** (*No. 3*) are among the buildings erected in what has become a thriving district in its own right. The square's "spiritual" centerpiece is the gleaming **Sony Center** (*www.sonycenter.de*), host venue for the world famous **Berlinale** film festival (see p. 102). Continuing the cinematic theme, the center's **Deutsche Kinemathek** (Film and Television Museum; see p. 29) presents an interactive look at the history of German cinema and TV. At the square's southwestern corner, the brown-brick **Kollhoff-Tower** *(No. 1)* boasts the fastest elevator in Europe (24 stories in 20 seconds), and it's a journey well worth making. A **Panoramapunkt** *(www.panoramapunkt.de, 030 25 93 70 80, €€, closed Dec. 24)* occupies the 24th and 25th stories of the building. Its 360-degree viewing platform promises views over the city as far as the eye can see. While here, you should also take a look at the venue's outdoor exhibition, which details the colorful history of the square.

Potsdamer Platz • www.potsdamerplatz.de • S-Bahn/U-Bahn: Potsdamer Platz

Checkpoint Charlie

5 Checkpoint Charlie was one of the most famous crossing points between East and West Berlin during the Cold War. Nowadays, the former checkpoint is still there—or at least an imitation of it—right down to the uniformed "guards" and a copy of the famous "YOU ARE NOW LEAVING THE AMERICAN SECTOR" sign. At the site, the **Mauermuseum: Museum Haus am Checkpoint Charlie** (Wall Museum: Museum House at Checkpoint Charlie; *www.mauermuseum.de, 030 25 37 250, €€€€*) emphasizes the "human freedom" aspect of the wall years. The museum showcases the creative ways in which East Berliners tried to escape the GDR (DDR) regime. Highlights include extraordinary personal tales and exhibits of hot-air balloons, vehicles with concealed compartments, and a one-man submarine. More general exhibits hinge on the concepts of freedom and nonviolent protest and include pages from Mohandas Gandhi's diary.

SAVVY **TRAVELER**

If you were expecting to see the real Checkpoint Charlie, you needn't be disappointed. The original is currently housed in Dahlem's **AlliiertenMuseum** (see pp. 160–161), among other exhibits from the postwar Allied occupation.

Friedrichstrasse 43–45 • U-Bahn: Kochstrasse

PalaisPopulaire

6 A place for interdisciplinary culture and a celebration of the contemporary in multiple styles, this gallery draws from Deutsche Bank's rich art collection and collaborates with museums, cultural institutions, and independent curators around the world. The palace also hosts sporting events, presentations, and readings with authors, artists, and prominent intellectuals. There is no shortage of educational activities for children and families, sometimes in English (check in advance on the website). The gallery's inaugural exhibition in September 2019 was dedicated to paper in art, followed by others that are always original and often harnessing the power of multiple languages: rock'n roll, dance-theater, land art, and more.

Unter den Linden 5 • www.db-palaispopulaire.de • 030 20 20 930 • €€ (temporary exhibitions) • Closed Tues. • U-Bahn: Unter den Linden

The Prinzessinnenpalais, vacant for years, is now the pleasant home of PalaisPopulaire.

Deutsches Historisches Museum

7 The German Historical Museum is housed in Unter den Linden's oldest building, a 300-year-old baroque armory. Spanning over 1,500 years of German history, the museum is organized chronologically and covers nine major eras from the early Dark Ages to the present day. To avoid feeling overwhelmed by the sheer volume of the 7,000 items on show, it is best to focus on just one or two eras—the Reformation and the Thirty Years' War, the days of the German Empire, the Weimar Republic, or Divided Germany, for example. Audioguides, available in English at the ticket office (€3), offer greater insight into a selection of highlights per era and help to build a picture of life in Germany at the time. Supplementing the permanent exhibition, an annex designed by architect I. M. Pei displays temporary shows throughout the year on subjects as diverse as the 1813 Battle of Leipzig or a retrospective of photojournalism in the former GDR (DDR).

Unter den Linden 2 • www.dhm.de • 030 20304 750 • €€ (temporary exhibitions) • Closed Dec. 24 • S-Bahn/U-Bahn: Friedrichstrasse

Neue Wache

8 The next-door neighbor of the Deutsches Historisches Museum facing Bebelplatz is the so-called New Guard. Karl Friedrich Schinkel's neoclassical guardshouse was originally built for the troops of the crown prince of Prussia and is now a monument dedicated to the victims of all wars. Step inside to see an enlarged version of Käthe Kollwitz's sculpture ***Mother With Her Dead Son.*** A shaft of light coming in through an oculus in the roof dramatically illuminates the sculpture on sunny days.

Unter den Linden 4 • U-Bahn: Unter den Linden

■ **ISHIN**
Boasting a spacious, unfussy interior, this is one of the best value-for-money restaurants in the area, and one of the only places to get really good sushi. **Mittelstrasse 24, 030 20 67 48 29, €€**

■ **LUTTER & WEGNER**
Overlooking Gendarmenmarkt, this restaurant serves refined German-Austrian food and has one of the best schnitzels in the city. There is a great wine list, which is also available if you dine at the adjacent bistro. **Charlottenstrasse 56, 030 20 29 54 15, €€€**

UNTER DEN LINDEN & AROUND

Bebelplatz

9 Bebelplatz is one of Unter den Linden's most handsome squares and the home of the famous National Opera House, the **Staatsoper**, reopened in 2017 after seven years of restoration. At the heart of the square, barely visible until you're almost on top of it, you'll find a memorial to the book burning of May 10, 1933. On that day the Nazis set fire to more than 20,000 "degenerate" works, including books by Thomas Mann, Heinrich Heine, and Karl Marx. The memorial, by Micha Ullman, consists of the subterranean, glass-covered **Leere Bibliothek**—an empty library with enough shelving to hold all 20,000 books. Set into the ground close by, you'll see an associated plaque bearing an engraving of a line from Heine, which translates as: "Where they burn books, they ultimately burn people." If you're visiting in summer, you may catch a free, open-air **Staatsoper für alle** concert, organized by the state opera company in June *(check website for details; www.staatsoper-berlin.de)*. Crowds of more than 30,000 people gather to enjoy this "opera for all."

Bebelplatz • U-Bahn: Hausvogteiplatz

Gendarmenmarkt

10 Two near-identical, 18th-century churches face each other at opposite ends of this opulent and lively square. The **Französischer Dom,** erected to serve the city's French Huguenot community, now houses a museum dedicated to Huguenot history— the **Hugenottenmuseum** *(www. hugenottenmuseum-berlin.de, €, closed Mon.)*. Come prepared to climb the 294 steps to the church's viewing platform (*franzoesischer-dom.berlin, €*) and you'll be rewarded with spectacular views. If you've no head for heights, but an interest in politics, the **Deutscher**

IN **THE KNOW**

Berlin's Mitte (center) can, depending on who you're talking to, refer to the trendy "downtown" section south of Torstrasse (known formerly as the Spandauer Vorstadt) or a broader area incorporating Alexanderplatz and Museumsinsel. The borough "Mitte" also includes Tiergarten and Wedding.

Schinkel's Konzerthaus (left) and the Französischer Dom (right) provide an elegant backdrop for the many visitors who come to the Gendarmenmarkt to socialize at the square's cafés.

Dom *(030 22 73 04 31, closed Mon.)* houses five stories of German parliamentary history. Between the two churches is the striking **Konzerthaus** *(www.konzerthaus.de),* built by royal architect Karl Friedrich Schinkel in 1821. Home to the Konzerthausorchester Berlin, it's one of the finest music venues in the city. Four main halls—sumptuously decorated in period style—host more than 500 concerts a year, from symphonies and chamber music to musical theater and children's concerts. In front of the entrance, stop to admire the **Schiller Monument** honoring the late 18th-century German *Sturm und Drang* (Storm and Stress) poet, Johann Christoph Friedrich von Schiller. Here, the poet stands above four allegorical figures sitting at his feet, each one representing an area of his work: history, lyric poetry, philosophy, and tragedy.

Gendarmenmarkt • U-Bahn: Hausvogteiplatz

Reichstag

Germany's national parliamentary building is a jewel in the crown of Berlin's 21st-century makeover.

The dome's mirrored sculpture reflects light into the parliamentary chambers below.

Destroyed by fire, devastated by Allied bombing during World War II, and ignored for decades by the Nazis and the former GDR (DDR; both of whom based their parliaments elsewhere), Germany's Reichstag (parliament) building has had it far from easy. British architect Sir Norman Foster added the iconic glass dome during his post-reunification refurbishment of the building. The dome, now a fixture on the Berlin skyline, has come to symbolize the progressive transparency of a reunited Germany.

OLD MEETS NEW

The Reichstag forms part of the **Regierungsviertel,** or Government Quarter—a string of buildings whose clean, modern lines and extensive use of glass reflect the openness and transparency of the modern government. On arrival, scrutinize the Reichstag's imposing neo-baroque exterior to see the 1916 inscription *Dem Deutschen Volke* (To the German People), as well as a number of bullet holes deliberately preserved as part of the old-meets-new restoration strategy.

On entering the building, see how its interior balances architectural glass-and-steel gestures with imposing Greek columns and preserved "victory graffiti" scribbled onto the walls by Soviet soldiers following the Battle of Berlin in 1945. Take the elevator to the roof terrace at the base of the dome.

BREAKFAST AT THE DOME

The Reichstag is the only parliament building in the world with a public dining area, but you need to book in advance to eat at the Käfer rooftop restaurant *(www.feinkost-kaefer.de, €€€)*. Try the breakfast, then sit back and enjoy the views from the terrace.

SAVVY **TRAVELER**

Visitors to the dome must register in advance. All tours are free and can be arranged at the nearby Service Center (beside the Berlin Pavilion on the south side of Scheidemannstrasse), but waiting times can be long. It is best to book online ahead of your trip.

A TOUR OF THE DOME

Inside the dome, a mirrored, cone-shaped light sculpture dominates the space. Around its base, you can read a short account of the building's history. Then peer down into the parliamentary debating chambers; the dome sits directly above them. Pick up a free audioguide when you are ready to climb the 755-foot-long (230 m) staircase that winds elegantly around the interior of the glass dome. Lasting 20 minutes and triggered by proximity sensors, the audioguide describes the dramatic and fascinating history of the building, including the time artists wrapped it entirely in polypropylene (1995). The guide also draws attention to a number of visible landmarks outside the building. Once at the top, you can enjoy the 360-degree panorama of the city.

Platz der Republik 1 • www.bundestag.de • 030 22 73 21 52 • Closed Dec. 24 • S-Bahn/U-Bahn: Brandenburger Tor

UNTER DEN LINDEN & AROUND

The Golden Twenties

The Berlin of the 1920s was modern and exciting. Home to many artists and writers, it was famous for its wild nightlife—the bars and cabarets immortalized in the film *The Blue Angel* and the musical *Cabaret*. Given the terrible loss of life in the preceding World War I and the horrors of World War II to follow, it is no surprise that this decade is fondly remembered as "The Golden Twenties."

M. Friedlaender's Berlin café scene captures the louche atmosphere of the city during the 1920s.
Opposite: Marlene Dietrich as Lola Lola in *Der blaue Engel* (*The Blue Angel*)

By November 1918, World War I was over, the Kaiser had abdicated, and revolution was in the air. A republic had been declared and a battle for power was underway. Elections held early in 1919 gave victory to the Social Democrats led by Friedrich Ebert. The government fled the maelstrom of Berlin politics for the relative safety of Weimar, 120 miles (193 km) to the southeast. The new Weimar Constitution, adopted in August 1919, was full of hope, optimism, and equality. But it was overly idealistic, for these were times of mass unemployment, widespread poverty, and rampant hyperinflation. The days were marked by riots, strikes, and street combat between the Nazis and the communists. This turbulence persisted: During the next 14 years there would be 17 changes of government and 13 chancellors.

Berlin entered a phase of liberalism in society and the arts, attracting young, fresh, and daring supporters. Unfettered by censorship, they were eager to explore and exploit Berlin's newfound freedoms. Among them was the dancer Anita Berber. A rising star of an avant-garde cabaret scene, Anita kept a suite

UNTER DEN LINDEN & AROUND

of rooms at the Hotel Adlon on Pariser Platz. After her evening performances she'd head for the five-star hotels on Unter den Linden, wearing an ankle-length sable coat that she dared the maitre d's to take to the cloakroom—she wore nothing underneath.

Come to the Cabaret

Cabaret thrived in many forms, with performers, composers, and lyricists becoming household names. They included openly lesbian singer Claire Waldoff, with her gruff persona and repertoire of 300 songs, as well as Margo Lion and a young Marlene Dietrich. Their flirtatious duet "Wenn die beste Freundin" ("When my Best Girlfriend") was a smash hit of the day. Clubgoers could see Trude Hesterberg, Kate

MARLENE **DIETRICH**

Born in the Schöneberg district of Berlin, Dietrich started her career in the chorus line, making her first stage appearance in 1922. She shot to international stardom following her leading role in *Der blaue Engel (The Blue Angel)*, the first major German talkie. At the time, producers and directors from Hollywood were flocking to Berlin's UFA studios, where cutting-edge techniques were being perfected. One producer, Josef von Sternberg, persuaded Dietrich to move to Hollywood with him, where she became an icon of the silver screen.

Kühl, or the outrageous Wilhelm Bendow. By 1925, Conrad Veidt, who had spent the first few years of the decade working the Ku'damm dressed as a girl, was Germany's highest paid film actor.

Berlin's nightlife attracted artists, writers, and performers from all over Europe, among them Erich Kästner, Klaus and Erika Mann, Jean Cocteau, André Gide, and Ernest Hemingway. Josephine Baker arrived from Paris in 1925, bringing "La Revue Negre" to the Theater des Westens. She became an overnight sensation. It was said that after seeing Baker, the women of Berlin were never the same again.

Christopher Isherwood (above left) moved to Berlin in the late 1920s. He was lured by descriptions of life in the city in letters he received from his school friend, the poet W. H. Auden (above right), who had been living in Berlin for eight months.
Opposite: Cover of *Lustige Blätter* magazine

A City of Women

For it *was* a city of women: World War I had wiped out a generation of men and boys. Women were wanted and needed in the workforce, giving them personal and financial freedoms they'd never experienced before. Working women had their own apartments, bank accounts, social lives, and wardrobes purchased at the newly affordable department stores springing up all over the city.

Writers and Artists

Bertolt Brecht lived in Schöneberg, where he wrote the lyrics for composer Kurt Weill's *Die Dreigroschenoper (The Threepenny Opera)*. A young British writer, Christopher Isherwood, arrived in March 1929. It was while living on Nollendorfstrasse that he recorded the events of everyday life in his diaries. Reworked as fiction, they'd become his two Berlin novels, *Mr Norris Changes Trains* and *Goodbye To Berlin*. The latter forms the basis of the stage and screen musical *Cabaret*, which introduced the world to Sally Bowles, a singer lost in the heady world of Weimar Berlin, portrayed on screen in 1973 by Liza Minnelli.

Dawn of Darkness

In Berlin, the only constant was change. A succession of failed governments gave rise to the far right. Banks collapsed and unemployment rose. Five general elections were held in 1932 against a backdrop of social reform that included a campaign to curtail what Berlin was most famous for—its wild nightlife. Clubs, bars, and cabarets were raided and those allowed to remain open had their opening hours reduced. At the end of January 1933, the elderly German President Paul von Hindenburg appointed Adolf Hitler as chancellor. The National Socialists were in power, and the Weimar Republic was finished.

THE REAL **WEIMAR**

For artists like George Grosz and Otto Dix the harsh realities of postwar Weimar society were all too real. In many of their works, Berlin life is depicted as sordid and seedy. Grosz's fat-cat businessmen and half-naked women wander dangerous streets, while Dix's *Portrait of the Dancer, Anita Berber,* painted in 1925, is now one of the most iconic images of the era. Here, the dancer poses with attitude and lips as red as the dress she wears.

Brunch

Many Berliners like to stay out into the wee hours and sleep late, so it's no surprise that brunch has a special place in their hearts. Virtually every neighborhood has a decent selection of brunch spots, ranging from traditional German platters to generous Russian, Italian, and Mediterranean buffets.

■ CAFÉ IM DEUTSCHEN HISTORISCHEN MUSEUM

Located separately from the main building at the German Historical Museum on Unter den Linden, this pleasant café has a spacious interior and a wonderful outdoor terrace that looks across the Spree River to the Berliner Dom. The menu focuses on regional dishes and local produce, with brunch options such as the "Zeughaus" (cheese and cold meats, smoked salmon, and boiled egg).

Unter den Linden 2 • www.dhm.de • 30 206 427 44 • €€ • U-Bahn: Unter den Linden

■ BARCOMI'S

This buzzy café and delicatessen is a perennial favorite with locals. Owned by American cookbook author Cynthia Barcomi, this place serves up breakfasts and bagels with an American twist, as well as a heavenly cheesecake and a great selection of house-roasted coffees.

Bergmannstrasse 21 • www.barcomis.de • 030 612 037 32 • € • U-Bahn: Gneisenaustrasse

■ CAFÉ IM LITERATURHAUS

Occupying a delightful turn-of-the-20th-century villa on an elegant side street off the bustling Ku'damm in Charlottenburg, this café-restaurant offers a fine menu for breakfast and lunch. The location is among the most pleasant in the area, with its lush garden and charming *wintergarten*—a true green oasis in the city.

Fasanenstrasse 23 • cafe-im-literaturhaus.de • 030 88 25 414 • € • U-Bahn: Uhlandstrasse

■ PASTERNAK

Located on the corner of a leafy square in Berlin's east, the quaintly atmospheric Pasternak serves the best Russian-themed Sunday brunch in the

UNTER DEN LINDEN & AROUND

Brunch at Café Bastard in Kreuzberg

city. From 9 a.m. the serving tables are filled with mountains of blinis, caviar, salmon, and exquisite desserts.

Knaackstrasse 22/24 • www.restaurant-pasternak.de • 030 441 3399 • € • U-Bahn: Senefelderplatz

■ CAFÉ BASTARD

This café *(currently under renovation, reopening scheduled in 2023)* is highly regarded for the quality of its coffee and breakfast. Fresh homemade bread baked on stone is served as an accompaniment. Extras include hard-boiled eggs and homemade jam.

Reichenberger Strasse 122 • www.bastard-berlin.de • € • U-Bahn: Kottbusser Tor

■ CAFÉ MORGENLAND

The weekend brunch in this Kreuzberg café is something of an institution. The Mediterranean-themed spread includes Middle Eastern and Turkish salads and stuffed vegetables as well as hummus, couscous, meatballs, eggs, freshly baked breads, homemade dips, and pancakes.

Skalitzer Strasse 35 • morgenland-berlin-de. webnode.com • 030 61 13 291 • € • U-Bahn: Görlitzer Bahnhof

Around Museumsinsel

Nestled between the Spree River to the east and the Spreekanal (canal) to the west, Museumsinsel (Museum Island) combines neoclassical architecture with a calm riverside ambiance and five outstanding museums. Between them, the museums house more than 2,000 years of history from around the world, and include such treasures as the Pergamon Altar from ancient Greece and a world-famous bust of the ancient Egyptian queen, Nefertiti. Opposite, where the Castle once stood, the Humboldt Forum is now an outstanding cultural venue. Within striking distance, Alexanderplatz holds an altogether different fascination. Its vast, windswept landscape punctuated by the space-age Fernsehturm (TV Tower) epitomizes Soviet bravado of the 1960s. Between Museumsinsel and Alexanderplatz lies the Nikolaiviertel—a cluster of streets with a number of small, but charming, sights.

○ **The Bode-Museum sits at the northern end of Museumsinsel, where the Spree River and Spreekanal converge.**

Around Museumsinsel

*Dazzling skyline views and the pick of Berlin's
top museums are the highlights of this compact tour.*

1 Pergamonmuseum (see pp. 74–75) Tour the
galleries of this museum dedicated to the ancient
worlds of the Middle East and marvel at their
treasures from antiquity. Head next door.

2 Neues Museum (see pp. 82–85) Admire
the architecture as well as the exhibits at
the New Museum. Take a break in the pretty
Pleasure Garden before continuing on Am
Lustgarten.

3 Berliner Dom (see pp. 75-76) Climb the
magnificent dome for views across central Berlin. From
Lustgarten cross Bundestrasse.

4 Humboldt Forum (see pp. 76–77) Be amazed by the
contrast of rigorous lines and baroque exuberance in the
foyer before visiting the exhibitions. Head east through
the Marx-Engels-Forum.

5 Alexanderplatz (see pp. 77–78) Take in the Soviet-
style features of this historic square and former GDR (DDR)
landmark before exiting the square on the southern side.

**AROUND MUSEUMSINSEL DISTANCE: 3 MILES (4.5 KM)
TIME: APPROX. 10 HOURS U-BAHN START: MUSEUMSINSEL**

AROUND MUSEUMSINSEL

Map labels:

0 200 meters
0 200 yards

TORSTRASSE
LINIENSTRASSE
AUGUSTSTR.
SCHEUNENVIERTEL
ORANIENBURGER STR.
Oranienburger Tor
Oranienburger Str.
FRIEDRICHSTR.
ZIEGELSTR.
TUCHOLSKY STR.
MONBIJOUPARK
Museumsinsel
Bode-Museum
Alte Nationalgalerie
MITTE
Pergamonmuseum
Friedrichstrasse
Neues Museum
UNIVERSITÄTSSTR.
CHARLOTTENSTR.
FRIEDRICHSTR.
Altes Museum
LUSTGARTEN
Museumsinsel
UNTER DEN LINDEN
Unter den Linden
BEHRENSTR.
FRANZÖSISCHE STRASSE

❿ Hackesche Höfe (see pp. 80–81) Unwind at this network of refurbished art nouveau courtyards housing galleries, restaurants, theaters, and more.

❾ Haus Schwarzenberg (see p. 80) Soak up the postwar atmosphere of this scruffy, unrefurbished courtyard and reflect on its small but powerful contents. You'll find the Hackesche Höfe next door.

❽ Zille Museum (see pp. 79–80) Chuckle over the satirical cartoons of much-loved illustrator Heinrich Zille. Return to Alexanderplatz and take Spandauer Strasse to Rosenthaler Strasse.

❼ Knoblauchhaus (see p. 79) Get a feel for life in Biedermeier Berlin. Continue on Poststrasse and head south on Propstrasse.

❻ Nikolaikirche (see p. 78) Sample the delights of the Nikolaiviertel, starting with its eponymous church. Walk to the southern end of Nikolaikirchplatz.

Pergamonmuseum

1 With three distinct and rich collections across as many interconnected floors, the Pergamon Museum is among the most visited museums in the city. Consider buying tickets online in advance (see sidebar opposite). There is a great deal to see here, although sadly the main attraction, the **Pergamonaltar** (Pergamon Altar), is out of action until 2024 owing to the reconstruction works involving the entire island. Disappointment will be short-lived, however, if you head straight for the Roman Art galleries and the **Market Gate of Miletus,** a 98.5-foot-wide (30 m) marble monument from the 2nd century A.D., with ornate friezes featuring bull and flower reliefs. The 46-by-98.5-foot (14 by 30 m) **Ishtar Gate**—the eighth gate to the inner city of Babylon (575 B.C.), once considered one of the Seven Wonders of the World—is another highlight. Besides these monumental exhibits, an impressively vast main hall hosts the **Antikensammlung**

A reconstruction of the Ishtar Gate, one of several gates to the ancient city of Babylon

(Collection of Classical Antiquities), some of which is also held in the Neues Museum (see p. 84) and in the Altes Museum. Among the exhibits here are sculptures, mosaics, pottery, and architecture from the archaic to Hellenistic ages. On the first floor, the **Museum für Islamische Kunst** (Islamic Art Museum) shows artwork from the 8th to the 19th centuries, including the **Mshatta Facade,** from the unfinished Mshatta palace located in present-day Jordan, or the impressive painted wooden paneling of the **Aleppo room.** Head down to the museum's basement for the **Vorderasiatisches Museum** (Middle East Museum), for objects found within areas of Assyrian, Sumerian, and Babylonian culture.

James-Simon-Galerie, Bodestrasse • www.smb.museum • 030 26 64 24 242 • €€€ • Closed Mon., Dec. 24, and 31 • U-Bahn: Museumsinsel

Neues Museum

2 See pp. 82–85.

James-Simon-Galerie, Bodestrasse • www.smb. museum • 030 26 64 24 242 • €€€ • Closed Mon. • U-Bahn: Museumsinsel

Berliner Dom

3 Modeled on St. Peter's in Vatican City, the exterior of the Protestant Berlin Cathedral, all ornate facades, granite stairs, and grandiose carved doors, is a blend of baroque and Italian Renaissance styles. No less dramatic on the inside, the cathedral's 230-foot-high (70 m) dome draws all eyes

SAVVY **TRAVELER**

Entry to Museum Island is free with the **Berlin WelcomeCard All Inclusive** or the **Museum Pass Berlin** (see p. 175). You can also buy tickets for individual museums online to book yourself into a specific time slot. Note that the island is undergoing reconstruction; check the shared website for developments.

All the museums share the same website, phone number, and weekly closing days (*www. smb.museum, 030 26 64 24 242, closed Mon., Dec. 24, and 31*).

Besides the **Pergamonmuseum** and the **Neues Museum,** the island boasts:

The **Alte Nationalgalerie** (Old National Gallery; *Bodestrasse,* €€€), with one of Germany's most significant collections of 19th-century art;

The **Altes Museum** (Old Museum; *Am Lustgarten,* €€€), with a wonderful rotunda as well as ancient artifacts from the Greek, Roman, and Etruscan eras;

The **Bode-Museum** (*Am Kupfergraben,* €€€), with a collection of art and artifacts from the Byzantine and medieval periods.

upward. Follow the "*Zur Kuppel*" signs to climb its 270 steps and you'll be rewarded with close-ups of the 500,000-piece mosaics portraying the beatitudes from the Sermon on the Mount. At the top, the views are breathtaking.

The nave is richly decorated, too. Of special note are pillars featuring the four main Protestant reformers (Luther, Melanchthon, Zwingli, and Calvin), reliefs illustrating the lives of the apostles, and a richly decorated chancel with an altar designed by Friedrich August Stüler. Admire the chancel's stained glass and oak pulpit. The **Sauer organ** is the largest late-Romantic organ in the world in its original condition and is a pleasure to hear—check the website for recital times, or purchase a recording in the cathedral.

The **Baptismal and Matrimonial Chapel** adjacent to the main hall contains a small museum that documents the building of the cathedral. In the crypt (*temporarily closed for renovation*) you'll find sarcophagi spanning 500 years, including those of 18th-century Prussian emperor Frederick I and his queen, Sophia. Outside, take a moment to enjoy the **Lustgarten** (Pleasure Garden), once a vegetable garden for the nearby Berliner Schloss (Royal Palace; see p. 119).

Am Lustgarten • www.berlinerdom.de • 030 20 26 91 36 • €€ (audioguide €4) • U-Bahn: Museumsinsel

Humboldt Forum

4 The combination of ancient and contemporary, as well as the idea of "connecting differences," were the guidelines for the realization of this Forum. Just look at the striking choices of Italian architect Franco Stella's design, a hymn to the cultures of the past and their dialogue with the present. The north, south, and west facades are a faithful reconstruction of those of the baroque

GOOD **EATS**

■ **CAFÉ OLIV**
This modern, airy café has a focus on organic and regional ingredients, and serves homemade sandwiches, soups, and delicious baked goods. **Münzstrasse 8, 030 89 20 65 40, €**

■ **ZUR LETZTEN INSTANZ**
Established in 1621, this is Berlin's oldest—and perhaps coziest—restaurant and once served Napoleon. The menu boasts traditional specialties such as grilled pork knuckle and Buletten (meat patties). **Waisenstrasse 14–16, 030 24 25 52 8, €€**

■ **ZUM NUSSBAUM**
A copy of one of the city's oldest pubs, this is a series of small, wood-paneled rooms. The menu features hearty German fare such as schnitzels, bockwurst, and potato salad. **Am Nussbaum 3, 030 24 23 09 5, €€**

Berlin Castle, bombed during World War II, while overlooking the Spree is a contemporary reinterpretation of them. Inside are numerous exhibition areas, an event stage, and more, giving maximum vent to the diverse and rich cultural offering of the city. In the foyer you will be welcomed by the "Kosmograf," a 56-foot-high (17 m) media tower that can turn into a giant art installation at any moment. Among the highlights inside are the **Berlin Ausstellung,** dedicated to the history of the city, and the **ethnological and Asian art collections,** among the world's best in their fields.

Schlossplatz • www.humboldtforum.org
• 030 99 211 89 89 • €€ (temporary exhibitions)
• U-Bahn: Museumsinsel

The Weltzeituhr in Alexanderplatz displays the time in major cities around the world.

Alexanderplatz

5 Just over a half a mile (1 km) east of Museumsinsel, yet a world away in terms of feel and architectural aesthetic, Alexanderplatz is one of Berlin's most historic squares and an important relic from the GDR (DDR) era. Often referred to simply as "Alex" by locals, the square is surrounded by the concrete *Plattenbauten* (modular high-rises) so typical of Soviet urban planning. A number of the square's communist-era structures have become protected landmarks, starting with the towering **Park Inn Hotel** *(No. 7),* the **Galeria Kaufhof** department store *(No. 9),* the **Brunnen der Völkerfreundschaft** (Fountain of International Friendship), all in the northwest corner, and on the other side the **Weltzeituhr** (World Clock), now a popular meeting point. South of here is the square's literal highlight, the 1,200-foot-tall (365 m) **Fernsehturm**

IN **THE KNOW**

The **Nikolaiviertel,** Berlin's historic center, underwent an intriguing architectural makeover during the former GDR (DDR) years. Rebuilt in 1987 to commemorate the city's 750th anniversary, the district aims to capture the aura of the Middle Ages and yet is built using the modular structures typical of East German architecture at the time.

(TV Tower; *Panoramastrasse 1a, www.tv-turm.de, 030 24 75 75 875, €€€€*), which features a rotating café-restaurant and a viewing platform with some of the best vistas in the city. To take a break from the square's Soviet-style architecture, step into the 13th-century **Marienkirche** (Church of St Mary; *Karl-Liebknecht-Strasse 8, www.marienkirche-berlin.de, 030 24 75 95 10*), beside the Fernsehturm, which boasts the 72-foot-long (22 m) "**Totentanz**" (Dance of Death) fresco, which dates back to the 15th century.

Between Karl-Liebknecht-Strasse and Rathausstrasse • U-Bahn/S-Bahn: Alexanderplatz

Nikolaikirche

6 The late-Gothic St. Nicholas's Church stands at the heart of the **Nikolaiviertel,** a reconstruction of Berlin's medieval oldtown. The oldest church in Berlin, it was originally built between 1220 and 1230, but suffered severe damage during World War II. No longer used for services, today the church functions mainly as a museum and, occasionally, a concert venue. As you walk around it today—inside and out—it is impossible not to admire its faithful restoration during the 1980s. To discover more on the history of the church, head for the broad Gothic nave and 15th-century ambulatory, home to a permanent exhibition on its history, complete with an interactive display. Parts of the church that did survive the war include a 14th-century bronze baptismal font and a handsome 18th-century pulpit. In the crypt you'll find a collection of medieval coins, graphic artworks, and medallions—lost during the war and recovered in the 1990s.

Nikolaikirchplatz 1 • www.stadtmuseum.de • 030 24 00 21 62 • €€
• U-Bahn: Klosterstrasse

Knoblauchhaus

7 Journey back in time to the Biedermeier era of the early 19th century with a tour of this former family home. The Knoblauchs were members of the new urban elite that came to define this period. Almost all of this three-story baroque town house erected in 1760 is original, making it one of very few such buildings still standing in Berlin today. It also housed the Knoblauch family business, which was connected to the silk industry. All of the rooms here feature original furnishings from the era—paintings, silverware, chandeliers, even a piano and an old bicycle—as well as pictures and documents that reveal elements of the Knoblauchs' privileged social lives in Berlin. While it is possible to visit the museum on your own, book in advance an hour-long tour in English to appreciate the full impact of the Biedermeier era on German society.

Poststrasse 23 • www.stadtmuseum.de/knoblauchhaus • 030 24 00 21 62 • Closed Mon. • U-Bahn: Klosterstrasse

Zille Museum

8 This small venue is dedicated to Heinrich Zille, a much-loved chronicler of Berlin's backstreets during the Weimar years—you'll pass a statue of the bearded artist as you approach. Once described by journalist Kurt Tucholsky as the "purest incarnation of Berlin," Zille's work often depicted the city's poorer inhabitants going about their daily lives. A permanent exhibition features

Heinrich Zille's skill lay in capturing the characteristics of Berlin's social stereotypes.

many original works, including his famous **Children of the Street** cartoons as well as paintings of prostitutes who used to work in nearby streets a century ago. Pop to the store for imaginative Zille-themed trinkets, postcards, and associated literature. Afterward, head to Zille's favorite *Kneipe* (bar), the nearby **Zum Nussbaum** (see sidebar p. 76).

Propststrasse 11 • zillemuseum-berlin.de • 030 24 63 25 00 • €€
• U-Bahn: Klosterstrasse

Haus Schwarzenberg

9 Schwarzenberg House is an unrefurbished courtyard with a compelling postwar aura, surrounded by small but significant museums that explore Jewish life during the Third Reich. The **Museum Blindenwerkstatt Otto Weidt** *(www.museum-blindenwerkstatt.de, 030 28 59 94 07)* is located in the workshop of Otto Weidt, who employed blind Jewish workers in his brush-making business. Weidt helped hide a number of his employees via a hidden room located behind a backless wardrobe. You can still see this room today, along with the rest of the workshop, which has been kept in its original condition. Farther toward the back of the courtyard is the **Anne Frank Zentrum** *(www.annefrank.de, 030 28 88 65 60 0, €€, closed Mon.),* which offers a modern, interactive exhibition exploring the life and experiences of Anne Frank, the Dutch teenage diarist whose family attempted to escape the Nazis by hiding in cramped rooms behind a concealed doorway at her father's warehouse in Amsterdam.

Rosenthaler Strasse 39 • S-Bahn: Hackescher Markt

Hackesche Höfe

10 Originally built in the 1900s and restored to its former art-nouveau glory in 1997, the distinguished Hackesche Höfe offers a stark contrast to **Haus Schwarzenberg**. This network of eight beautifully tiled and often ivy-clad courtyards *(Höfe)* is packed with places to shop, drink, eat, and people watch. Deserving special mention, **Endellscher Hof** is the first courtyard as you enter from Rosenthaler Strasse. Designed by August Endell, it features the **Chamäleon Theater** *(chamaeleonberlin.com)*, housed in an original tavern and offering everything from tap dancers to trapeze artists, and the **Hackescher Hof Restaurant** *(www.hackescher-hof.de, 030 28 35 293)*, which has a beautiful original ceiling. The other courtyards are home to fashion boutiques, gift shops, and handicraft stores. Most of them stay open up to 9 p.m., which adds to the unique, up-tempo evening vibe of the area. Browse some local favorites: **Trippen** *(Hof 4, www.trippen.com)*, the last word in avant-garde shoes; or **Coy Art to Wear** *(Hof 8, 030 65 79 84 96)*, with original hats designed by Cornelia Plotzki. Round off your day with cocktails at **Oxymoron** *(Hof 1, www.oxymoron-berlin.de, 030 28 39 18 86)*.

Rosenthaler Strasse 40–41 • S-Bahn: Hackescher Markt

Diners enjoy the laid-back atmosphere of the Endellscher Hof as passersby come and go.

Neues Museum

Ancient Egypt and early European history are the focus of this stunningly renovated venue on Museumsinsel.

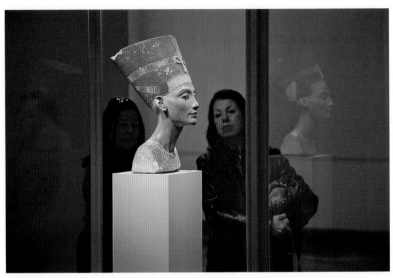

Among the museum's most prized possessions is this ancient bust of Nefertiti.

Berlin's Neues Museum is both an architectural and a cultural attraction. Built in the 1850s, it suffered severe damage during World War II. Now fully renovated, today's incarnation incorporates many remnants from the original building, intricately melding the old with the new. The rooms, in part inspired by ancient Egyptian, Greek, Roman, and Byzantine designs, vary hugely, from square to circular, domed to vaulted, and are now peppered with a dizzying array of cultural treasures and historical curiosities.

■ MAIN HALL

You enter the museum via the vast, showstopping **James-Simon-Galerie,** a modern take on the classical colonnade that opened in 2019 and has already won an architectural award. Right after that, the majestic **Vestibule** is a medley of old, exposed brickwork, new installations of concrete and marble, and a timber roof. The main wings of the building lead off from either side of this hall and surround two interior courtyards—the Greek and the Egyptian. Immediately opposite the entrance a grand staircase leads down to Level 0 with access to the Greek Courtyard, and up to Levels 2 and 3.

■ GREEK COURTYARD

Extending to the full height of the museum, this courtyard lies at the center of its southern wing. Look up to see enormous busts of the ancient Greek god Zeus and goddesses Hera and Athena peering back down at you. The main feature here is the 19th-century **Schievelbein Frieze,** which graces all four walls of the courtyard, and in which you can follow the violent eruption of Mount Vesuvius in 79 A.D. and the subsequent destruction of Pompeii.

■ EGYPTIAN MUSEUM AND PAPYRUS COLLECTION

Housed in the museum's northern wing and starting on Level 1, this collection holds some 2,500 artifacts, prefaced by a thorough historical overview of the collection and the discipline of Egyptology itself (Room 111). As you walk from one room to the next, note the boldly painted walls and ceilings—all remnants of the original interior. Highlights of the collection include the **Berlin Green Head** (Room 109)—a 400 B.C. head of a priest carved from smooth green stone. The climax of the collection, however, is the 3,330-year-old **bust of Nefertiti,** the wife of the legendary pharoah Akhenaten, who reigned ca 1353–1336 B.C. Although the bust is displayed in a room of its own on Level 2 (Room 210), be prepared to jostle for a decent view of it. It is worth doing so, though, particularly as photography of the piece is strictly prohibited.

■ EGYPTIAN COURTYARD

At the center of the northern wing, this courtyard is similar in size to the Greek Courtyard, and access can be gained on all three levels. Of particular note is Level 1, which seeks to re-create the atmosphere of an Egyptian temple. Here are the remains of four murals from the original museum—ten others were destroyed during the war—depicting scenes from Karnak, Edfu, the island of Philae, and Abu Simbel. Head down to Level 0 to see 13 stone sarcophagi or up to Level 2 for treasures from the reign of Akhenaten.

■ MUSEUM OF PRE- AND EARLY HISTORY

With 6,000 objects on view, the **Museum für Vor- und Frühgeschichte** occupies the southern wing of the museum. It offers a sweeping survey of archaeological finds from across Europe and parts of Asia from the Stone Age up to the Middle Ages, as well as objects from the **Antikensammlung** (an important collection of Greek and Roman antiquities; see also p. 75). On Level 1, there is an entire cabinet full of what looks like rubble (Room 102). As you get closer, you'll see the twisted, fractured, and in part molten remains of artifacts that were among the thousands of treasures destroyed in Allied bombing raids in 1945. Additional highlights of this collection include Heinrich Schliemann's collection of **artifacts from Troy** (the so-called Priam's Treasure, Rooms 103–104) and a cultural history of neighboring **Cyprus** (Room 106).

Highlights on Level 2 include an ancient Roman bronze statue of the **Xanten Youth** (Room 201) and an immense statue of the **ancient Greek sun god Helios** from the 2nd century A.D. (Room 203). This last is the only exhibit occupying the beautiful, three-story, brick-walled **Southern Dome Room.**

■ LEVEL 3

Up on the third floor, you'll find an exhibition dedicated to archaeological excavations in Berlin, with artifacts from the Stone Age, Bronze Age,

A vase depicting the Egyptian god Bes, ca 1550–1070 B.C.

Looking down at the stone sarcophagi in Level 0 of the Egyptian Courtyard

and Iron Age. Among the highlights of the Stone Age is an elk found at Berlin's Hansaplatz in 1956 (Room 308), whose existence testifies to the dramatic climate change that occurred during that period. From the Bronze Age you will find the world-renowned **Berlin Golden Hat** (Room 305)—a conical item made of thin gold leaf that represents one of four similar items known from Bronze Age Europe. Displays from Iron Age cultures have their own highlights, including Hallstatt-period graves (Room 302). If you have time for one exhibit only, head straight for the **"Time Machine"** river landscape (Room 304), where animated film sequences illustrate the lives of inhabitants from the landscape during the course of the preceding millennia. Created especially for the exhibition, the film includes many objects that feature in the museum's displays.

James-Simon-Galerie, Bodestrasse • www.smb.museum • 030 26 64 24 242 • €€€ • Closed Mon., Dec. 24, and 31 • U-Bahn: Museumsinsel

Jewish Heritage

In 1945, barely a trace of the capital's Jewish heritage had survived. What the Nazis hadn't destroyed had been obliterated by Allied bombing. And yet Jewish Berlin survives today with the golden dome of the city's restored Neue Synagoge, on Oranienburger Strasse, one of the dominant sights of Berlin's skyline. Berlin also has one of the world's fastest-growing Jewish communities.

The placard pictured was erected at the Jewish Tietz store, Berlin, during the 1933 Nazi boycott of all things Jewish. It reads, "Germans, defend yourselves. Do not buy from Jews."
Opposite: The Neue Synagoge on Oranienburger Strasse

A Troubled History

Jews first settled in Berlin in the 13th century, and endured centuries-long cycles of repression. From the end of the 17th century, increasing toleration saw a steady increase to the city's Jewish population. By the 19th century, Berlin had become a center for liberal Jewish thinking, and at the turn of the 20th century, there were more than 100,000 Jews in Berlin. The Weimar Era that followed World War I saw a cultural renaissance in the capital. Jewish politicians, writers, artists, and musicians were at the forefront of this cultural life. By this time, German Jews were largely middle class and well integrated in society. However, Berlin was also home to significant numbers of Eastern European Jews who had fled their shtetls because of pogroms. In stark contrast, these Jews were poor, ghettoized, and spoke Yiddish.

Descent into Barbarity

When the Nazis came to power in 1933, Berlin had around 160,000 Jews. By 1939, 75,000 of them had been driven abroad. Another 8,000 managed to survive the Holocaust, hidden by their fellow citizens in attics and basements. For many, however, there followed the well-documented passage to the death camps through detention centers such as the Jewish Old People's Home on Grosse Hamburger Strasse and the railroad station at Grunewald.

Jewish Berlin Today

After 1945, few of those German Jews who did survive the Holocaust chose to remain in Berlin, and it was not until the end of the Cold War that the city's Jewish population began to rise again, partly owing to influxes from Eastern Europe and the former Soviet Union. Testimony to Berlin's thriving Jewish community today are its synagogues and Jewish schools, cultural centers, and restaurants.

STOLPER**STEINE**

Memorials can be found throughout Berlin and include **Places of Remembrance** in Schöneberg (see pp. 142–143). Perhaps most touching, however, are Gunter Demnig's *Stolpersteine* (Stumbling Blocks). Found throughout Nazi-occupied Europe, these small brass squares are set into sidewalks, each one a memorial to a Jewish inhabitant who perished during the Holocaust. Seven such memorials lie at the entrance to the **Hackesche Höfe** (*Rosenthaler Strasse 40–41*), in memory of Anita Bukofzer, Ury and Paula Davidson, and the Schneebaum family, who all died at Auschwitz.

The Riverside

Berlin's two primary rivers—the Spree and the Havel—are supplemented by a multitude of smaller canals and lakes to create a network of inner-city waterways that crisscross the city. Along the banks you'll find pleasant boat rides, waterfront dining, and a host of other outdoor activities.

■ BEST RIVER CRUISE

One of the most enjoyable ways to see the main sights of Berlin is by river. Berliner Wassersport und Service GmbH & Co. (BWSG) offer a one-hour cruise aboard an open-topped boat. The tour starts and ends at the Alte Börse pier, in the Museumsinsel neighborhood; book early morning or late afternoon to avoid the midday sun.

The tour heads east first, offering a dramatic close-up of the nearby **Berliner Dom** (see pp. 75–76) and tantalizing glimpses of the medieval **Nikolaiviertel** (see p. 78). Turning at the Mühlendamm lock, the boat returns past the striking neoclassical facade of the **Alte Nationalgalerie** (see p. 75) and the distinctive dome of the **Bode-Museum** (see p. 75), before passing by Friedrichstrasse and the former Berlin Wall checkpoint. Cruising past the **Reichstag** (see pp. 62–63), the tour then breezes by some of the modernist architecture of the Government Quarter and on to the glass-and-steel Hauptbahnhof (train station), where—if you booked the evening cruise and it's sunny—you'll see crowds enjoying the sunshine, music, and drinks at the **Capital Beach Bar** (see p. 168). The boat continues to the **Tiergarten** (see pp. 98–99), before puttering pleasantly back to the starting point.

Burgstrasse 27 • www.bwsg-berlin.de • 030 65 13 415 • €€€€ • Closed early Nov.–end March • U-Bahn: Museumsinsel

■ BEST KAYAK TOUR

Kayak Berlin Tours run several types of paddling tour throughout the city, including Night Tours, Standup Paddleboarding Tours, and one in Potsdam.

www.kajakberlintours.de • 0179 12 42 924 • €€€€€

Cruising past the Hauptbahnhof, with Spreebogenpark in the foreground

■ BEST RIVERSIDE CLUB

Berghain, in Berlin's east, might be the most famous club in town, but **Watergate** in the Kreuzberg neighborhood is certainly one of the best-looking. Party into the early hours in the club's main room, with glitzy LED ceiling and big-name house and techno DJs. To chill out, head straight for the outdoor terrace where you can enjoy a drink while looking out across the Spree River and views of **Oberbaumbrücke** (see p. 90).

Falckensteinstrasse 49 • www.water-gate.de • 030 61 28 03 94 • €€ • Closed Mon.–Wed. • U-Bahn: Schlesisches Tor

■ BEST RIVERSIDE DINING

Set on a moored Dutch sailing boat on a section of the Spree River in the Kreuzberg neighborhood, **Van Loon** *(Carl-Herz-Ufer 5, vanloon.de, 030 69 26 293, €€)* is a charming spot for riverside drinks, a leisurely breakfast, or an al fresco dinner. For something more upscale, try the **Grill Royal** *(Friedrichstrasse 105b, grillroyal.com, 030 28 87 92 88, €€€€€)*, a high-end steakhouse near Museumsinsel. It's popular with a well-heeled crowd and has a pleasant outdoor terrace that looks out over the Bode-Museum and the Spree River.

The giant "Molecule Man" sculpture rising from the Spree River

■ BEST RIVERSIDE VIEW

One of the city's most handsome bridges, the **Oberbaumbrücke** also has an illustrious history. Linking Kreuzberg and Friedrichshain across the Spree River, the bridge began life as a timber bridge in 1724, became a Cold War landmark during Berlin's division, and has starred in Hollywood movies like *The Bourne Supremacy.* Today, the bridge's arches and pseudo-medieval turrets offer great views along the Spree River in both directions.

Intersection of Warschauer Strasse and Mühlenstrasse • U-Bahn: Schlesisches Tor

■ BEST RIVERSIDE STATUE

It's hard to miss **"Molecule Man"**—the iconic 98-foot-tall (30 m) aluminum landmark by American sculptor Jonathan Borofsky—in Berlin's east. Three figures lean toward each other as if for mutual support, providing a symbol of togetherness for the reunited city.

An den Treptowers 1 • S-Bahn: Treptower Park

■ BEST RIVERSIDE ACCOMMODATIONS

There are great options for an overnight stay on the water. The most fun is the **Eastern Comfort**

Hostelboat (*Mühlenstrasse 73, www.eastern-comfort.com, 030 66 76 38 06, €–€€*), which offers simple single, double, and four-person cabins and a basic breakfast. It's located right next to the **East Side Gallery** (see p. 129) and the Oberbaumbrücke.

■ BEST RIVERSIDE FLEA MARKET
Every two weeks, on a Sunday morning, the section of the Maybachufer that lines the Landwehrkanal in the Kreuzkölln district comes alive with the buzzy **Nowkölln Flowmarkt** (*www.nowkoelln.de*), a flea market that sells secondhand wares and design objects from local and international creatives. The market alway draws a youthful, happening crowd.

■ BEST BEACH BAR & POOL
The **Badeschiff** swimming pool is built from a recycled cargo container and floats right in the Spree River in Berlin's east. Conceived by local artist Susanne Lorenz, it's part of the sprawling Arena complex, which also features event venues, an open-air bar, and a sunbathing area. The venue has a beach with its own bar during summer.

Eichenstrasse 4 • www.arena.berlin • 030 53 32 030 • €€ • U-Bahn: Schlesisches Tor

Twilight on the banks of the Spree River, overlooking the Badeschiff

Tiergarten & Around

Dominated by the park from which it takes its name, this neighborhood has a unique—and particularly verdant—character. The Tiergarten itself is bisected by the majestic, tree-lined Strasse des 17. Juni.

A number of significant cultural venues flank the park, including the Neue Nationalgalerie, the Berliner Philharmonie, and the Bauhaus-Archiv to the south and the Haus der Kulturen der Welt (House of World Cultures) to the north, each designed by a leading architect of the 20th century. The buildings epitomize modern European architecture and—with contents that range from paintings by the old masters to seminal works from the Bauhaus movement—they contribute to this area's reputation as one of Berlin's primary cultural hubs.

◀ **A number of pretty bridges cross the waterways that converge at Tiergarten See in the southern section of the park.**

Tiergarten & Around

This leisurely stroll in historic hunting grounds is bracketed by the best of west Berlin's architectural and cultural sights.

5 **Tiergarten** (see pp. 98–99) Hofjägerallee will take you to the Victory Column for great views across the park. Explore any one of the several walking trails, before crossing Strasse des 17. Juni on the way to the park's northernmost flank.

6 **Haus der Kulturen der Welt** (see p. 99) Admire the exterior of this building—dubbed the "pregnant oyster" owing to its idiosyncratic shape— before stepping inside for a wide range of events, concerts, and exhibits from around the world.

TIERGARTEN & AROUND DISTANCE: 3 MILES (4.5 KM) TIME: APPROX. 9 HOURS S-BAHN/U-BAHN START: POTSDAMER PLATZ

1 **Gemäldegalerie** (see pp. 100–101)
View the esteemed collection of European artworks spanning 500 years at Berlin's Picture Gallery—one of several highlights at the city's Kulturforum. You'll see the Neue Nationalgalerie across the square. Stroll south and then east past Matthäuskirche to reach it.

2 **Neue Nationalgalerie**
(see pp. 96–97) This celebrated example of Bauhaus architecture, another gem at the Kulturforum, contains an array of masterpieces from the 20th century. Walk along Sigismundstrasse and then turn left on Stauffenbergstrasse.

3 **Gedenkstätte Deutscher Widerstand**
(see p. 97) DIscover the heroic stories of those who opposed the National Socialist regime. Take Sigismundstrasse back to the Landwehrkanal and walk along it to Klingelhöferstrasse.

4 **Bauhaus-Archiv** (see p. 97–98) The wavy-roofed building of the Bauhaus Archive will soon return to house exhibits from the seminal movement's leading designers, as well as an associated library. During the renovation works, a temporary archive is accessible. Head north on Klingelhöferstrasse and into the Tiergarten.

TIERGARTEN & AROUND

Gemäldegalerie

1 See pp. 100–101.

Matthäikirchplatz 4–6 • www.smb.museum • 030 26 64 24 242 • €€ • Closed Mon., Dec. 24, 31 • S-Bahn/U-Bahn: Potsdamer Platz

Neue Nationalgalerie

2 Known popularly as Berlin's "temple of light and glass," the New National Gallery was completely renovated and revamped from 2015 to 2021 by David Chipperfield Architects. The building boasts 54,000 square feet (5,000 sq m) of exhibition space. Its modern, clean-lined exterior—designed by Bauhaus affiliate Ludwig Mies van der Rohe—houses an extensive collection of European paintings and sculptures from the 19th century to the 1960s. The collection is displayed on a rotating basis and always includes works from major artists, including Picasso, Dalí, and Klee. On permanent display are the works of Die Brücke (The Bridge) movement, a group of German Expressionists that included Karl Schmidt-Rottluff, Erich Heckel, and

Seminal works of 20th-century European art are on display at the Neue Nationalgalerie.

Ernst Ludwig Kirchner. Don't miss Kirchner's "Potsdamer Platz," depicting the square as it was in 1914, before it was bombed in World War II. Currently under construction next to the Neue Nationalgalerie, the new 20th Century Museum is set to open in 2026.

Potsdamer Strasse 50 • www.smb.museum • 030 26 64 24 242 • €€ • Closed Mon., Dec. 24, 31 • S-Bahn/U-Bahn: Potsdamer Platz

Gedenkstätte Deutscher Widerstand

③ The German Resistance Memorial Center occupies the headquarters of the military plot that attempted to assassinate Hitler on July 20, 1944. It includes a museum that gives voice to individual or organized actions against Nazism in the years 1933–45. As of 2018, it also houses the **Gedenkstätte Stille Helden** (*www.gedenkstaette-stille-helden.de, 030 26 3989 0822*), which commemorates the "silent heroes" who put their lives on the line to save Jews.

Stauffenbergstrasse 13-14 • www.gdw-berlin.de • 030 26 99 50 00 • Closed Jan. 1, Dec. 24–26, 31 • S-Bahn/U-Bahn: Potsdamer Platz

Bauhaus-Archiv

④ Housed in a somewhat idiosyncratic building featuring a flotilla-shaped roof (designed by Bauhaus founder Walter Gropius), this museum is one of the best places in the world to get a sense of the breadth and depth of the Bauhaus movement. The main building is currently closed for renovation and expansion; when completed, it will house an archive, a library, and a store, while the new spaces, designed by Berlin-based firm Staab Architekten, will be the museum. Beneath the promenade level, in the shadow of an ethereal glass tower, the collection will find a new home, with classics

GOOD **EATS**

■ **FACIL**
This sophisticated Michelin-starred restaurant, set in the Mandala Hotel, is run by celebrated chef Michael Kempf. As well as high-end food, it offers splendid views from its fifth-floor dining room. **Potsdamer Strasse 3, 030 59 00 51 23 4, €€€€€**

■ **KIN DEE**
An awarded Thai restaurant, from the Royal Grill group. Excellent, authentic cuisine, based on local products from eco-friendly companies. **Lützowstrasse 81, 030 21 55 294, €€€€€**

■ **TEEHAUS IM ENGLISCHEN GARTEN**
A romantic, lakeside restaurant in the Tiergarten whose bistro-style dishes include soups, stews, and burgers. **Altonaer Strasse 2, 49 30 39 48 04 00, €€**

TIERGARTEN & AROUND

This Tiergarten statue depicts a family of lions, the lioness wounded by an arrow.

such as Wilhelm Wagenfeld's lamp and Marcel Breuer's Wassily chair, some beautifully minimal armchairs and desks from Mies van der Rohe, paintings by Josef Albers and Paul Klee, wallpaper design, and chess sets (don't miss Josef Hartwig's oak, maple, and pear set, with each piece designed to reflect the moves it makes in the game). Larger items will include a curvaceous coffee bar, designed for the 1930 Werkbund Exhibition in Paris. Although the **Temporary Bauhaus-Archiv** in Charlottenburg (*Knesebeckstrasse 1-2*) does not display the collections, it hosts the shop and events on design-related topics.

Klingelhöferstrasse 14 • www.bauhaus.de • U-Bahn: Nollendorfplatz

Tiergarten

5 The former hunting ground of the Great Elector Friedrich Wilhelm (1620–1688), the Tiergarten (Animal Garden) is one of Berlin's largest green spaces. Spanning more than 500 acres (200 ha), these green lungs contain almost 16 miles (25 km) of footpaths skirting a variety of lakes and ponds, gardens and meadows, with a wide choice of picnic and barbecue spots, cafés, and beer gardens in which to while away the afternoon. At the heart of the park—halfway along its main axis, Strasse des 17. Juni—stands the **Siegessäule** (*Grosser Stern 1, €*). This column, topped in 1864 with a gilded statue of the goddess of victory, was erected in celebration of Prussian military success against the Danes. Climb the stairs to the top for views over the park and the city. North of here lies the elegant **Schloss Bellevue,** built in 1786 for Prince August Ferdinand and now the official residence of the German president. At the eastern end of Strasse des 17. Juni stands the **Sowjetisches Ehrenmal** (Soviet Memorial), an immense bronze statue of a soldier. It was built to commemorate Soviet victory over the Nazis during the Battle of Berlin (May 1945). The T-34 tanks that flank the monument are said to be the very ones that first fought their way into the city.

Strasse des 17. Juni • S-Bahn: Tiergarten

Haus der Kulturen der Welt

6 Located on the Spree River to the north of the Tiergarten, the House of World Cultures—with its dramatically sweeping roof and curvaceous facade—is fronted by an equally striking bronze sculpture by Henry Moore. Originally designed as a congress hall in 1957, the building was a gift from the United States and symbolized the freedom of West Berlin. Explore the expansive interior to find an auditorium, an exhibition hall, a roof terrace, and a number of smaller areas for concerts and theater projects. These spaces are used for themed events, exhibitions, festivals, lectures, and concerts—many with free admission—that focus on the culture and society of non-European nations (check the website for details).

John-Foster-Dulles-Allee 10 • www.hkw.de • 030 39 78 70 • €–€€€ • Closed Tues. (exhibitions only) • U-Bahn: Bundestag

SAVVY **TRAVELER**

If you are visiting Berlin in the summer, time your walk in the Tiergarten to coincide with a free concert at the **Teehaus im Englischen Garten** (see sidebar p. 97). Live music fills the air on Sundays at 4 p.m. and 7 p.m. from June through September.

Gemäldegalerie

The works of Brueghel, Dürer, Rubens, Rembrandt, and more jostle for wall space at Berlin's Picture Gallery.

Early works include Pieter Brueghel the Younger's "Carrying the Cross" (ca 1606).

With more than 1,000 works on view at a time—about half of those available—this collection of old masters constitutes one of the finest in Europe. It includes portraits, genre paintings, decorative panels, interiors, landscapes, and still lifes. Among the works are a number amassed by both the Great Elector Friedrich Wilhelm and Frederick the Great. The German and Dutch masterpieces from the 15th to the 17th centuries, and Italian collections from the 13th to the 16th centuries are particularly impressive.

■ WANDELHALLE

The rooms in this gallery are arranged around a vast central foyer—the Wandelhalle—and are organized geographically as well as chronologically. They follow a quirky numbering system—the bigger rooms have Roman numerals, while others use Arabic. The Wandelhalle has been recently renovated to offer exhibitions that approach the museum's works from different points of view; at its center is a fountain installation by American artist Walter De Maria.

■ GERMAN AND FLEMISH WORKS

Rooms dedicated to German and Flemish works boast masterpieces that include **"Portrait of a Young Venetian Woman"** (1506) by Albrecht Dürer (Room 2); **"Altar with the Last Judgment"** (1524) by Lucas Cranach (Room III); **"Dutch Sayings"** (1559) by Pieter Brueghel the Elder (Room 7); and 16 Rembrandts, including a compelling self-portrait from 1634 (Room X).

■ ITALIAN WORKS

Key highlights in the Italian Renaissance section include no fewer than five different Madonnas by

SAVVY **TRAVELER**

On display in the **Bode-Museum** (see sidebar p. 75) are some 200 paintings from the Gemäldegalerie specifically chosen to interact with the sculptures preserved there. There is also a long-term project to transfer the gallery's entire holdings to the Museumsinsel in the future.

Raphael (Room 29). Collectively, they demonstrate the painter's progression in confidence and style from his early work to his time in Florence. Additional Italian masterpieces include such famous works as Caravaggio's **"Love Conquers All"** (1602), Botticelli's **"Portrait of a Lady"** (1460–1465), and Correggio's **"Leda and the Swan"** (ca 1530), the famous depiction of the popular Greek myth, in which the god Zeus takes the form of a swan in order to seduce a young woman.

■ A CLOSER LOOK

For a detailed study of some of the more prominent paintings on display, you'll find a **digital gallery** with computer guides on the lower floor (accessed by stairs from Room XV).

TIERGARTEN & AROUND

Matthäikirchplatz 4–6 • www.smb.museum • 030 26 64 24 242 • €€ • Closed Mon., Dec. 24, 31 • S-Bahn/U-Bahn: Potsdamer Platz

Cultural Capital

With the fall of the wall, newly united Berlin became Germany's cultural as well as governmental capital. Today, it offers classical events alongside a thriving avant-garde scene. Like so much in Berlin, the city's cultural identity is rooted in the events of the last 100 years—from the decadence of the 1920s arts scene to the legacy of the divided city to its current role as national capital.

The Berlin International Film Festival draws audiences of half a million every year and previews as many as 400 films. Opposite: Concertgoers enjoy a classical concert at Berlin's Philharmonie.

Cultural Divisions

In divided Berlin, both sides used culture as a form of propaganda. East Berlin offered world-class opera and concerts with tickets one-tenth the price of those in New York and London. In West Berlin, the glamorous **Berlinale** *(www.berlinale.de)* was launched in 1951 and remains a mainstay of the city's cultural calendar. A move in the 1960s to create a new cultural hub in a bombed-out area of West Berlin near the wall resulted in the **Kulturforum** with its showpiece architecture by Mies van der Rohe and Hans Scharoun. It includes museums, libraries, and the **Berliner Philharmonie** *(www.berliner-philharmoniker.de)*, Berlin's premier venue for classical music.

Arts at the Cutting Edge

The Berlin tradition of artistic experimentation that emerged after World War I (see pp. 64–67) continues thanks in part to the city's many vacant industrial buildings, which give dancers, artists, and creative types the space to create large-scale works. For example, **Radialsystem V** *(Holzmarktstrasse 33, www.radialsystem.de, 030 28 87 88 50)* is housed in a converted water-pumping station on the banks of the Spree River, and provides innovative performances, family-friendly events, and a relaxing riverside terrace.

On Stage

Unsurprisingly, in the city that inspired Bertolt Brecht, theater is important to Berlin's cultural life. The **Deutches Theater** *(Schumannstrasse 13a, www.deutschestheater.de, 030 28 44 12 25)* has occupied the same building since 1883, while the **English Theatre Berlin** *(Fidicinstrasse 40, www.etberlin.de, 030 69 35 692)* works in English, for them the lingua franca of the 21st century.

BERLIN **ON CELLULOID**

Few capital cities have inspired the film industry as much as Berlin has. Explore the city on the silver screen with **The Blue Angel** (1930) starring Marlene Dietrich (see sidebar p. 65), Billy Wilder's **One, Two, Three** (1961), Wim Wenders's **Wings of Desire** (1987), Tom Tykwer's **Run Lola Run** (1998), and Wolfgang Becker's **Good Bye, Lenin!** (2003).

TIERGARTEN & AROUND

City Parks

Berlin is one of Europe's greenest cities, with a wealth of public spaces available for strolling, sunbathing, and sports. Many parks share characteristics with the city's largest—the Tiergarten (see pp. 98–99)—and are home to a number of significant memorials, museums, and more.

■ SPREEBOGENPARK

This park, landscaped in 2005, nestles into a bend in the Spree River in the northwestern corner of the Tiergarten neighborhood. Sandwiched between two bridges, the park has split-level walkways planted with boxwood and riverside grasses. They provide great views of central Berlin and direct access to the waterfront.

Ludwig-Erhard-Ufer • U-Bahn: Bundestag

■ MONBIJOUPARK

Once the grounds of Monbijou Palace, this small park located opposite **Museumsinsel** (see pp. 70–91) is perfectly located for taking a break from sightseeing. It's especially good for kids, thanks to the two pools (swimming and paddling) and an ice-cream kiosk. There are also benches and trees for shade.

Monbijoustrasse • S-Bahn: Hackescher Markt

■ TEMPELHOFER PARK

Bridging the Schöneberg and Kreuzberg neighborhoods, this defunct airport—expanded into its current format by the Nazis—was proclaimed a public space in 2010. The former runway is a particularly popular spot for kite-surfing, cycling, and in-line skating. Among the park's diverse attractions you'll find everything from a **Shaolin temple** and community gardens to sculptures by local artists and official grilling areas. Parts of the former **Flughafen** (airport buildings) can also be accessed by several different guided tours (see website for details) and are sometimes used for major events, such as the annual **Berlinale** (see p. 102), or as a movie and photoshooting set.

Entry: Tempelhofer Damm, Columbiadamm, Oderstrasse • www.thf-berlin.de • 030 20 00 37 400 • S-Bahn/U-Bahn: Tempelhof

Kite-surfing on the former runway at Tempelhofer Park

■ MAUERPARK

Formerly the site of the Berlin Wall and its associated Death Strip, Wall Park in Berlin's east became a community park in the early 1990s. Flanked to the east by Friedrich-Ludwig-Jahn Sports Stadium (remnants of the former wall can still be seen at the top of the embankment here), the park occupies a special place in the hearts of Berliners. A neighboring area hosts a flea market on Sundays (see p. 153) and an amphitheater that is home to popular karaoke sessions in summer (see p. 171).

Bernauer Strasse • U-Bahn: Bernauer Strasse

■ TREPTOWER PARK

Dominated by the 24-acre (10 ha) **Soviet Memorial** that commemorates the death of the 20,000 Russians who died in the Battle of Berlin, Treptower Park in Berlin's east also offers a promenade along the Spree River, leafy woods, and a pleasant **Karpfenteich** ("carp pond"). You can also visit the **Archenhold-Sternwarte** observatory (*Alt-Treptow 1, www.planetarium.berlin, 030 53 60 63 719, closed Mon.–Thur.*), where Einstein gave his first public lecture on his theory of relativity.

Alt-Treptow • S-Bahn: Treptower Park

CHARLOTTENBURG

Charlottenburg

Historically one of Berlin's wealthiest neighborhoods, Charlottenburg evolved into a major cultural hub during the Weimar era, brimming with bars, galleries, department stores, and cabarets. During the years of division, the area maintained its commercial feel, and remains one of the best parts of the city for shopping, as well as sightseeing. Its main street, Kurfürstendamm (or Ku'damm for short), is Berlin's answer to the Champs-Elysées in Paris and London's Oxford Street. This large-scale, leafy boulevard is lined with leading fashion stores and restaurants, while its elegant side streets are home to clusters of antique dealers, independent boutiques, and more. Nearby sights include Berlin's prestigious royal residence, Schloss Charlottenburg—from which the neighborhood takes its name—the war-torn tower of Kaiser Wilhelm Memorial Church, and the deeply thought-provoking Käthe-Kollwitz-Museum.

CHARLOTTENBURG

◀ **The lavish interior of the Golden Gallery at Schloss Charlottenburg**

NEIGHBORHOOD **WALK**

1 **Schloss Charlottenburg** (see pp. 114–117)
Allow three hours to explore the many rooms
and wonderful gardens of this former royal
residence. Walk south on Kaiser-Friedrich-
Strasse to Adenauerplatz.

SCHLOSSGARTEN
CHARLOTTENBURG

Belvedere

Mausoleum

Schloss
Charlottenburg

Neuer
Pavillon

Altes Schloss

1

Neuer Flügel

Orangerie

Gipsformerei

2 **Käthe-
Kollwitz-Museum**

SPANDAUER DAMM

2 **Käthe-Kollwitz-
Museum** (see pp. 110–111)
This museum provides
an insight into the
pacifist artist's work
and life. Return to
Ku'damm and continue
east to Breitscheidplatz.

KLAUSENERPLATZ

Westend

OTTO-SUHR-ALLEE

Richard-
Wagner-Platz

SCHLOSSSTRASSE

DANCKELMANNSTRASSE

SCHUSTEHRUS-
PARK

CHARLOTTENBURG

ZILLESTRASSE

KAISER-FRIEDRICH-STRASSE

CAUERSTRASSE

LEIBNIZSTRASSE

SOPHIE-
CHARLOTTE-
PLATZ

Bismarckstrasse

BISMARCKSTRASSE

Deutsche
Oper

SCHILLERSTRASSE

Sophie-
Charlotte-
Platz

| 0 | 500 meters |
| 0 | 500 yards |

3 **Kurfürstendamm** (see p. 111)
Discover the myriad shops,
galleries, and museums on both
sides of this famous and eternally
busy boulevard. Halfway along,
head south on Fasanenstrasse.

**CHARLOTTENBURG DISTANCE: 3.5 MILES (5.6 KM) TIME:
APPROX. 10 HOURS U-BAHN START: RICHARD-WAGNER-PLATZ**

CHARLOTTENBURG

Charlottenburg

Combine the riches of Prussian luxury with a good shopping spree in Berlin's royal neighborhood.

4 Kaiser-Wilhelm-Gedächtnis-Kirche (see pp. 112–113) You'll see the broken spire of Kaiser Wilhelm Memorial Church and its adjacent modern buildings to the north of Ku'damm. Inside are exhibitions as well as elements of religious and architectural interest. Walk east on Tauentzienstrasse toward Wittenbergplatz.

5 KaDeWe (see p. 113) A short stroll east on Tauentzienstrasse will bring you to Wittenbergplatz and one of Europe's largest department stores: KaDeWe, with a plethora of excellent brands for all occasions. The top floors are a foodie paradise.

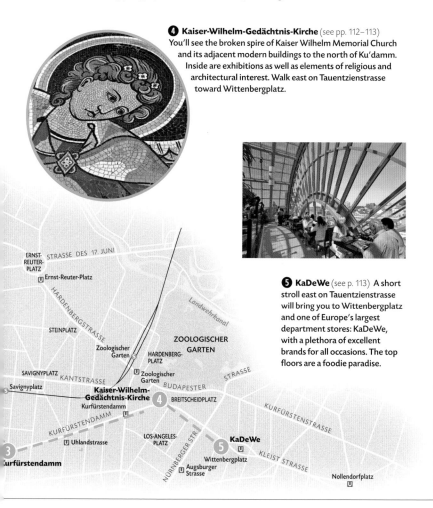

Schloss Charlottenburg

1 See pp. 114–117.

Spandauer Damm 10–22 • www.spsg.de • 03 31 96 940 • €€€€ • Closed Mon., Dec. 24, 25 • U-Bahn: Richard-Wagner-Platz

Käthe-Kollwitz-Museum

2 Recently moved to the Theaterbau in Schloss Charlottenburg, this museum hosts an extensive collection of works by one of Berlin's most famous 20th-century female artists. With charcoal sketches, woodcuts, lithographs, and sculptures, the permanent exhibition reflects Kollwitz's status as a lifelong pacifist dedicated to campaigning against war and suffering. The collection features early political works such as "A Weavers Uprising" (1893–1897) and "Peasants' War" (1902–1908), and striking posters created in 1924 for International Workers Aid, bearing potent titles such as "Germany's Children Are Starving!," "Bread!," and "Never Again

Kurfürstendamm is Berlin's answer to the Champs-Elysées in Paris.

War!" Perhaps the most poignant though, are the sketches and sculptures that Kollwitz created during the outbreak of World War I, to which she lost a son. Their heartbreaking titles— "Widowed Orphans," "Killed in Action," and "Survivors"— say it all.

Spandauer Damm 10 • www.kaethe-kollwitz.de
• 0049 30 882 5210 • €€ • Closed Dec. 24, 31
• U-Bahn: Richard-Wagner-Platz

Kurfürstendamm

3 Charlottenburg's main boulevard, Kurfürstendamm, is known as Ku'damm for short and offers a mix of high-end fashion boutiques, chain stores, and classy restaurants. The most exclusive stores lie at the western end, where you'll find the likes of **Chanel** *(No. 188–189)*, **Yves Saint Laurent** *(No. 52)*, and **Louis Vuitton** *(No. 185)* interspersed with chic boutiques that include haute couture store **Harveys** *(No. 56, harveys.berlin, 030 88 33 803)*, ladies emporium **Veronica Pohle** *(No. 64, www.veronicapohle.de, 030 88 33 73 1)*, and quality shoe store **Budapester Schuhe** *(No. 43, www.mybudapester.com, 030 88 62 42 06)*. For a break from shopping, head to the **Story of Berlin** *(No. 206–209, www.story-of-berlin.de)*. Temporarily closed, this exhibition on eight centuries of the city's history will be remounted in the Fürst complex, which will reopen in 2023 in the same spot. Stroll into Ku'damm's eastern environs for medium-priced international fashion chains and sport brands, as well as around 70 shops located in the **Europa-Center** *(Breitscheidplatz, www.europa-center-berlin.de)*.

East-west axis between Joachim-Friedrich-Strasse in the west and Tauentzienstrasse in the east • U-Bahn: Adenauer Platz

GOOD **EATS**

■ **BIER'S KUDAMM 195**
If you are tempted to try currywurst (see sidebar p. 113), try it here, at one of the only spots in the city that sells the famed fast food as well as champagne. **Kurfürstendamm 195, 030 88 18 94 2, €**

■ **CAFÉ IM LITERATURHAUS**
Enjoy lunch, dinner, or just *Kaffee und Kuchen* at this elegant café in a pleasant villa next to the Käthe-Kollwitz-Museum. If it's sunny, grab a seat in the garden. **Fasanenstrasse 23, 030 88 25 41 4, €€**

■ **PARIS BAR**
A central hub for the former West Berlin's prolific art scene until the wall fell, there's still something enjoyably bohemian about the Paris Bar and its reliable French menu. **Kantstrasse 152, 030 31 38 05 2, €€**

CHARLOTTENBURG

The Kaiser-Wilhelm-Gedächtnis-Kirche was built to glorify the first emperor of the unified Germany.

Kaiser-Wilhelm-Gedächtnis-Kirche

4 Located at the eastern end of **Ku'damm** (see p. 111), what remains of the late 19th-century Kaiser Wilhelm Memorial Church is one of west Berlin's most dramatic sights. All but destroyed during World War II, the base of the old spire (deliberately left bomb-damaged) and vestibule of the original church now serve as a **Hall of Remembrance.** Here, you'll find display panels documenting the church's history and its destruction, through photos, historical illustrations, artifacts, and objects that survived the bombing. A number of restored mosaics include one on the floor that depicts Archangel Michael fighting the dragon.

The modern buildings on this site were designed by celebrated German architect Egon Eiermann in the 1950s. They include the octagonal **Neue Kirche** and the **Neuer Turm** (New Church and Tower). Step into either and savor the impact made by the stained glass. There are 21,000 individual panes—almost all of them blue. Additional sights within the church include an aluminum baptismal font filled with marble pebbles and a dramatic mechanical organ. Look above the altar to see a sculpture of Christ made from tombac—a brasslike alloy of zinc and copper. See how it glows against the blue of the stained glass. On the northeastern wall are three artworks: Kurt Reuber's charcoal "Stalingrad Madonna," drawn in 1942 and placed here as a reminder of the deaths of hundreds of thousands of soldiers on both the German and Russian sides; a bronze plaque commemorating Protestant martyrs under the Nazi regime (see if you can spot the 13th-century Spanish crucifix); and an icon of the Virgin Mary from Volgograd. An adjacent 174-foot (53 m) tower contains a belfry with six bronze bells that chime on the hour. The church holds music services on Saturdays (*6 p.m.*).

Breitscheidplatz • www.gedaechtniskirche-berlin.de • 030 21 85 02 3 • U-Bahn: Kurfürstendamm

KaDeWe

5 Formally known as the Kaufhaus des Westens (Department Store of the West), but abbreviated to KaDeWe, this shopper's paradise is one of the largest in continental Europe. Expect the place to be busy—you'll be one of the thousands of visitors who come here daily. Each of the store's eight floors is arranged around a retail theme: beauty products and luxury goods, men's attire, women's fashion, children, and so on. If you're a foodie, take an elevator straight to the seventh floor, where dozens of gourmet counters serve everything from currywurst to imported Italian delicacies. The top floor also has a 1,000-seat, glass-fronted restaurant and winter garden with great views over the city.

Tauentzienstrasse 21–24 • www.kadewe.de • 030 21 210 • U-Bahn: Wittenbergplatz

Overlooking the central hall at KaDeWe. The store first opened its doors in 1907.

CHARLOTTENBURG

Schloss Charlottenburg

Experience the luxuries of life enjoyed by the royal inhabitants of this opulent Prussian palace.

The majestic facade of the Old Palace at Schloss Charlottenburg

Schloss Charlottenburg is the largest remaining royal residence in the German capital. Former residents of the Old Palace building include Queen Sophie Charlotte, second wife of Friedrich I, king of Prussia, in the early 1700s, and Friedrich II (Frederick the Great) in the 1750s. A visit to this site and its landscaped gardens—studded with flower beds, statues, and several notable buildings—provides a compelling insight into the courtly life of Brandenburg-Prussia from the baroque period right up until the early 20th century.

■ ALTES SCHLOSS

You access the Old Palace (€€€, closed Mon.) via the **Great Courtyard,** with its equestrian statue of Friedrich Wilhelm I, son of Friedrich I. Before entering the building, admire the monumental 165-foot (50 m) domed tower, added between 1710 and 1712, which can be seen for miles around.

The first room you enter displays photographs of how the palace looked directly after World War II—that is, largely devastated—and underlines how much of the opulence that follows is due to careful restoration. Only a smattering of the interiors, antiquities, and artworks scattered throughout the bedrooms, beauty rooms, studies, and audience chambers survived the bombings; the rest were drafted in from former Prussian palaces elsewhere, including the **Berliner Schloss** (see sidebar p. 119).

Among the many exquisite treasures on both floors are paintings and portraits of the palace's previous inhabitants and their royal relatives and esteemed friends. Some rooms boast entire walls of damask and original writing desks, others have beautiful tapestries and French-style ceiling frescoes. One room even has an original white harpsichord that was played by Sophie Charlotte.

SAVVY **TRAVELER**

Schloss Charlottenburg is best seen on a self-guided tour. Expect to spend at least three hours here. While the palace gardens are free to enter, each of the individual buildings has a separate entrance fee. Purchase a day card (€€€€) that allows you access to all of the buildings. Start at the Altes Schloss and the Neuer Flügel, then see how much time you have left for the other sights.

Don't miss the dazzling **Porzellankabinett** (Porcelain Cabinet; Room 95), one of the oldest and largest of its kind in Germany, which contains some 2,700 items of exquisite chinoiserie, and the new permanent exhibition dedicated to the Hohenzollern dynasty, featuring the magnificent **crown jewels,** including the golden crowns of Friedrich I and Sophie Charlotte.

The palace's west wing features the **Grosse Orangerie** (Great Orangerie). Mainly used for cultural events and classical concerts today, this extension was originally to be mirrored on the eastern side of the building, but Frederick the Great had other plans.

■ NEUER FLÜGEL

In place of the proposed orangerie, Frederick the Great added a rococo New Wing (€€€, closed Mon.) to the eastern side of the Altes Schloss. The first section of the building was finished in 1742, with rooms designed by royal architect Georg Wenzeslaus von Knobelsdorff, while the upper floor was designed mainly by Johann August Nahl. Most of the highlights are, in fact, upstairs. They include—to the left at the top of the stairs—the flamboyant banqueting hall, called the **Weisser Saal** (White Hall). Beyond that is the **Goldene Galerie** (Golden Gallery), a 138-foot-long

Exquisite stuccoed walls with gilt decoration at Schloss Charlottenburg

(42 m) ballroom with mesmerizing aquamarine walls. Within the king's private chambers is an important rococo painting by Antoine Watteau, **"Einschiffung nach Cythera"** ("Pilgrimage to Cythera"), ca 1718.

■ NEUER PAVILLON
Just beyond the Neuer Flügel is the New Pavilion (€€, closed Mon.). Built by Prussian architect Karl Friedrich Schinkel in 1825 as a summer retreat for King Friedrich Wilhelm III, this charming Italianate villa was reconstructed in 1970. The former rooms, arranged on two stories around an elegant staircase, exhibit paintings, furniture, works of art, and porcelain from the "Schinkel era." Stop to admire romantic landscapes by Schinkel himself—a gifted painter as well as architect—and his contemporaries Caspar David Friedrich, Karl Blechen, and Eduard Gärtner.

■ SCHLOSSGARTEN
The Palace Gardens are one of the venue's real highlights. Reflecting different periods of the palace's history, the section directly behind the **Altes Schloss** (see p. 115) follows the original, geometric planting plan (designed after the French model), while the rest retains the late 18th- and

The immaculately tended baroque-style Schlossgarten

early 19th-century restyling, which follows the less formal English model. Heading north through the gardens, you'll first come across the neoclassical **Mausoleum** *(€, closed Nov.–March and Mon. year-round)*, built in 1810 to house the tomb of Queen Luise. You'll also find the marble sarcophagi of other members of the royal family here, such as Queen Luise's husband, King Friedrich Wilhelm III, and Kaiser Wilhelm I and his wife, Augusta. Still heading north, the pretty, three-story **Belvedere** *(temporarily closed)* sits on the banks of the Spree River. Designed by Carl Gotthard Langhans, architect of the **Brandenburger Tor** (see p. 54), the belvedere was initially conceived as a teahouse for Friedrich Wilhelm II. Its somewhat unexpected contents include a world-renowned collection of porcelain—wall fittings, decorative vases, statuettes, dinner services, and tea sets of various Prussian kings—all made by Berlin's royal manufacturer KPM (Königliche Porzellan-Manufaktur, or the Royal Porcelain Manfacturers).

Spandauer Damm 10–22 • www.spsg.de • 03 31 96 940 • €€€€ • Closed Mon., Dec. 24, 25 • U-Bahn: Richard-Wagner-Platz

Royal City

Berlin's great royal age began in 1701, when Friedrich III, Duke of Prussia, had himself crowned Friedrich I, King of Prussia. He brought together five towns—Berlin, Cölln, Friedrichswerder, Dorotheenstadt, and Friedrichstadt—to form the capital and royal residence of Berlin. From that time until the end of the monarchy in 1918, Berlin benefited from a number of royal patrons.

**A champion of the Enlightenment, Frederick the Great studied music and French literature, and even wrote and composed several works himself.
Opposite: Prinz-Heinrich-Palais at the Forum Fridericianum in a lithograph by W. Loeillot, ca 1840.**

Frederick's Forum

Friedrich I's grandson, Friedrich II (Frederick the Great, 1740–1786), shaped the Berlin cityscape that we see today. One of his first projects, started in 1741, was the Forum Fridericianum, designed by architect Georg Wenzeslaus von Knobelsdorff in a mix of architectural styles (neoclassical, baroque, rococo) as a new scientific center and artistic focal point for the Prussian Kingdom. Built around the former Opernplatz (today's **Bebelplatz;** see p. 60), the Forum included the Staatsoper, St. Hedwig's Cathedral, the Zeughaus, Kronprinzenpalais, Opernpalais, and Prinz-Heinrich-Palais.

Art and Science

The **Altes Museum** (see sidebar p. 75), the first museum built in Berlin, was constructed in 1830 by Karl Friedrich Schinkel. But it was romanticist Friedrich Wilhelm IV (1840–1848) who dedicated the **Museumsinsel,** originally a residential area, to "art and science" in 1841. He personally commissioned the **Alte Nationalgalerie** and the **Neues Museum** (see pp. 82–85). All the important city architects—Schinkel, Langhans, Knobelsdorff, and Nering—were involved in the construction of the island.

The Last Kaiser

Wilhelm II (1888–1918) was famous for his conservative tastes and hatred of anything "modern." His favorite architect was Ernst von Ihne, whose major buildings include the neo-Romanesque **Kaiser-Wilhelm-Gedächtnis-Kirche** (see pp. 112–113). He also famously lined a Tiergarten path leading up to the **Siegessäule** (see p. 99) with bland statues of former kings—a move that was sarcastically dubbed the *"Puppenallee"* ("street of the dolls") by locals. Germany's defeat in World War I led to revolt against the monarchy, and Kaiser Wilhelm II was Germany's last royal patron.

BERLINER SCHLOSS

The Prussian monarchy's winter residence, the **Berliner Schloss,** was first built on **Museumsinsel** in 1443. It underwent modifications and expansions over the centuries, the most significant starting in 1701 with Frederick I: Thanks to the most important architect of the time, Andreas Schlüter, the castle became one of the most spectacular Baroque mansions in Europe. Heavily damaged during World War II, it was demolished in 1950. In 2012, work began that led to the opening in December 2020 of the current **Humboldt Forum** (see pp. 76–77).

Christmas Markets

With roots in the late Middle Ages, the German Christmas market has long been a fixture of the festive season. Throughout Advent, markets big and small switch on their fairy lights and fill the air with the enticing smells of cookies, sausages, and Glühwein. Dates vary year to year, so check websites for details.

■ SCHLOSS CHARLOTTENBURG
One of Berlin's most romantic markets takes place on the grounds of **Schloss Charlottenburg** (see pp. 114–117), where you'll find more than 150 stalls, many inside heated tents and elegant glass pagodas. On-site entertainment includes Ferris wheels, live music, choirs, and a children's market with its own carousel and petting zoo. The palace gardens are illuminated especially for the event.

Spandauer Damm 10–22 • U-Bahn: Richard-Wagner-Platz

■ GENDARMENMARKT
Set between the beautiful domes of the **Deutscher Dom** and **Französischer Dom** on **Gendarmenmarkt** (see pp. 60–61) in the Unter den Linden neighborhood, this market offers a dizzying array of stalls and activities. Culinary delights are supplied by upmarket establishments such as **Galeries Lafayette** and **Lutter & Wegner,** as well as the usual crêpe and grill stalls. There are also lots of high-end artisanal gifts to buy and a weekend stage program hosting everything from fire artists to gospel singers.

Gendarmenmarkt • www.gendarmenmarkt berlin.de • € • U-Bahn: Hausvogteiplatz

■ OPERNPALAIS
Officially titled the "Nostalgic Christmas Market," this event at the Opernpalais on Unter den Linden offers a program of live music, family activities, and an art exhibition. There are more than 150 stands selling everything from roast chestnuts to South Tyrolean specialties, fairground carousels for kids, and romantic carriage rides for adults.

Unter den Linden • U-Bahn: Hausvogteiplatz

CHARLOTTENBURG

Irresistible Christmas goodies at the Gendarmenmarkt

■ RIXDORFER WEIHNACHTSMARKT

Another unique experience can be found nestled in the heart of trendy Kreuzkölln on the fringes of the Kreuzberg neighborhood. Quaint at the best of times, with its medieval houses and cobbled streets, the small bohemian village of Rixdorf takes on an extra-nostalgic hue for three days at the beginning of December, with market stalls hawking handmade goods, local schnapps, special pony rides around the stables, and demonstrations by blacksmiths.

Richardplatz • U-Bahn: Karl-Marx-Strasse

■ LUCIA WEIHNACHTSMARKT
   AT THE KULTURBRAUEREI

This Scandinavian-themed market takes place in the handsome cobbled courtyard of the **Kulturbrauerei** in Berlin's eastern district of Prenzlauer Berg (see p. 126). Named after the Nordic goddess of light, the market includes plenty of Nordic-themed stalls selling things like Norwegian punch, specialty chocolates, and designer housewares. There are plenty of food and gift stalls, kids' rides—and even a sauna.

Schönhauser Allee 36 • www.lucia-weihnachts markt.de • U-Bahn: Eberswalder Strasse

Berlin's East

Every city has its "east side," but Berlin's has the distinction of having also been the capital of an entirely different country for several decades. The erection of the Berlin Wall in 1961 meant that the city's eastern districts suddenly found themselves part of the GDR (DDR) until reunification in 1990. This half of the city subsequently developed in a distinctly different direction to its western counterpart, architecturally, socially, and politically.

The post-reunification frenzy of cultural and commercial activity in the former GDR (DDR) districts of Mitte, Prenzlauer Berg, and Friedrichshain resulted in rampant regeneration of Berlin's east. Today, the overriding character of this neighborhood is one of trendy residential areas defined by broad, cobbled streets, 19th-century housing, and a slew of upscale cafés, restaurants, and boutiques. Explore a little farther, however, and you'll find fascinating remnants of the area's communist past.

◄ **The redbrick turrets**
of Oberbaumbrücke
rise above what's left
of the Berlin Wall at
the East Side Gallery.

❶ Gedenkstätte Berliner Mauer
(see pp. 130–131) **Visit Berlin's most poignant memorial to those who fell at the Berlin Wall. Walk east on Oderberger Strasse.**

❷ Kulturbrauerei
(see p. 126) **Explore the neighborhood's 19th-century industrial roots with a visit to this former brewery, now a cultural complex with shops, a cinema, and live music venues. Walk south on Knaackstrasse.**

BERLIN'S EAST

❸ Kollwitzplatz (see p. 127) **Stop for lunch in or around handsome Kollwitzplatz. Walk southeast on Wörther Strasse, then Marienburger Strasse, and finally Hufelandstrasse to reach Am Friedrichshain.**

BERLIN'S EAST DISTANCE: 7 MILES (11.5 KM)
TIME: APPROX. 8 HOURS S-BAHN START: NORDBAHNHOF

Berlin's East

*Pretty residential streets and reminders of the Cold War
define this tour of Berlin's eastern districts.*

6 **East Side Gallery** (see p. 129) Staying on Mühlenstrasse, view the largest open-air gallery in the world. The vivid display of street art harks back to the fall of the Berlin Wall in 1989.

5 **Karl-Marx-Allee** (see p. 128) Admire the Soviet architecture of this monumental boulevard. Take the bus (No. 142) heading south to the U-Bahn stop. Get off at Ostbahnhof for a short walk south to Mühlenstrasse.

4 **Volkspark Friedrichshain** (see p. 128) Enter the park at Virchowstrasse and explore its 128 acres (52 ha) with special areas for climbing, jogging, and skateboarding. Exit at Friedenstrasse and head south to Platz der Vereinten Nationen, then take Lichtenberger Strasse to Strausberger Platz.

Map labels:
GENSLER-STRASSE
ENTRALFRIEDHOF FRIEDRICHSFELDE
ICHTENBERG
Lichtenberg
Friedrichsfelde
IEDRICHS-FELDE
Betriebsbahnhof Rummelsburg

Once a thriving brewery, the Kulturbrauerei is now a multivenue entertainment and culture center.

Gedenkstätte Berliner Mauer

1 See pp. 130–131.

Bernauer Strasse 111 and 119 • www.
berliner-mauer-gedenkstaette.de • 030 21
30 85 123 • Visitor Center closed Mon.
• S-Bahn: Nordbahnhof

Kulturbrauerei

2 This red-and-yellow-brick complex once functioned as one of the most important breweries in Berlin. Dating back to 1842, the 6-acre (2.5 ha) site was refurbished during the 1990s into an entertainment and culture complex. Its various buildings are now occupied by an array of cafés, shops, restaurants, and clubs. In summer, its handsome cobbled courtyards host events like children's fairs and classical concerts. The popular **Nordic-themed Christmas Market** (Lucia Weihnachtsmarkt; see p. 121) takes place here in winter.

On arrival, make for the permanent **"Alltag in der DDR"** exhibition ("Everyday in the GDR"; *Knaackstrasse 97, www.hdg.de, 030 46 77 77 9-11, closed Mon.*), which displays original objects, documents, films, and audio recordings from the days of East Germany. Afterward, browse eco-furniture at **Green Living** (*030 9561 0061*) and, if you happen to visit on a Sunday, check out the lively **Street Food Market**. The brewery's former boiler house, the **Kesselhaus**, is one of Berlin's best music venues and attracts an impressive lineup of rock, pop, jazz and blues bands. There are no contact details online, so drop by to see what's on during your stay.

Schönhauser Allee 36 • www.kulturbrauerei.de • U-Bahn: Eberswalder Strasse

Kollwitzplatz

3 The beating heart of trendy Prenzlauer Berg, this vibrant square is named after celebrated artist Käthe Kollwitz, who lived in the area at the turn of the 20th century. A haven for young families, the square has three separate playgrounds and a leafy park. It's surrounded by rows of refurbished 19th-century houses, whose ground floors contain numerous bars and cafés. There is barely any traffic, and you could happily stop for a drink while the children play. This is a great spot for a little laid-back shopping—at **Mundo Azul** *(Choriner Strasse 49)* you will find children's books in several languages, while **OYE Records** *(Oderbergerstrasse 4)* offers new and used vinyl records. On Saturdays the square hosts a farmers' market, while Thursdays are dedicated to local organic produce. On these days the square is a little busier than usual (see p. 153).

Kollwitzplatz • U-Bahn: Senefelderplatz

BERLIN'S EAST

Children play at one of several fun playgrounds at the center of Kollwitzplatz.

GOOD **EATS**

■ **SCHÖNBRUNN**
Set in a former-GDR (DDR) pavilion in Volkspark Friedrichshain, this café and restaurant serves Austrian-Mediterranean cusine. **Am Schwanenteich im Volkspark Friedrichshain, 030 45 30 56 52 5, €€**

■ **GUGELHOF**
This Kollwitzplatz favorite serves traditional food from the Alsace region, including *Flammkuchen* (tarte flambée). **Knaackstrasse 37, 030 44 29 22 9, €–€€**

■ **KANAAN**
Genuine Middle Eastern Israeli cuisine, such as you might find in Jerusalem, with many vegetarian and vegan options. **Schliemannstrasse 15, 030 45 95 6801, €€**

Volkspark Friedrichshain

4 The Friedrichshain People's Park is second only in size to the Tiergarten (see pp. 98–99). Focus your visit on two outstanding memorials from the GDR (DDR) era. As you enter the park you'll see the twin columns of the **Memorial to Polish Soldiers and German Anti-Fascists,** which celebrates the communist resistance fighters who joined forces against National Socialism. On leaving the park, on Friedenstrasse, don't miss the **Memorial to the International Brigades in the Spanish Civil War,** honoring the communist volunteers who fought for the Republic in the Spanish Civil War (1936–1939). Stylistically, these sculptures epitomize the socialist realism that pervaded all communist culture during the Cold War years.

Am Friedrichshain 1 • U-Bahn: Strausberger Platz

Karl-Marx-Allee

5 Conceived by the GDR (DDR) as a flagship of postwar Soviet architecture, 2-mile-long (3.2 km) Karl-Marx-Allee was constructed during the 1950s and 1960s. Imposing, Soviet-style apartment houses line the boulevard. Head straight for **Café Moskau** *(No. 34),* a treasure trove of Soviet art and sculpture—from its modernist structure to the socialist-realist mosaic gracing its facade and the *Sputnik* model zooming into the sky above it. Across the boulevard, the modernist cinema, **Kino International** *(No. 33),* designed by the same architect (Josef Kaiser), is no less impressive in its embodiment of the Soviet modernist style.

Karl-Marx-Allee • U-Bahn: Strausberger Platz

East Side Gallery

6 Stretching 0.8 mile (1.3 km) along Mühlenstrasse on the east bank of the Spree River, the East Side Gallery is the longest remaining section of the Berlin Wall. It features more than 100 paintings by artists from all over the world, most of whom came to daub their satirical comments onto the concrete slabs when the gallery opened in 1990. Highlights include German artist Birgit Kinder's painting of a Trabant breaking through the wall and Russian artist Dmitri Vrubel's portrait of communist leaders Honecker and Brezhnev sharing their legendary kiss. Since 2016, the **Wall Museum** (*Mühlenstrasse 78-80, thewallmuseum.com, 030 94 51 29 00, €€€*) has complemented the open-air gallery with interviews and exhibits about the Wall years and the impact it had on the lives of Berliners. Beyond the wall you'll see the redbrick towers of **Oberbaumbrücke.** This bridge served as a Berlin Wall border crossing during the Cold War and, as such, marks a fitting end to this tour of Berlin's east.

Mühlenstrasse • www.eastsidegallery-berlin.de • U-Bahn: Warschauer Strasse

Dmitri Vrubel's painting bears the caption: "My God, help me to survive this deadly love."

Gedenkstätte Berliner Mauer

*A stretch of the former Berlin Wall now serves as
a dedicated Berlin Wall Memorial.*

The Window of Remembrance shows the faces of those who fell trying to escape.

This memorial to the Berlin Wall stretches the entire 0.87-mile length (1.4 km)
of Bernauer Strasse and is by far the best site from which to appreciate the
physical and psychological effects of one of the most brutal divisions of the
20th century. The East–West border dissected Bernauer Strasse in two,
separating neighbors on one side of the street from those on the other. Today,
steel poles have replaced the wall, marking out its original path. They lead you
north, from one exhibit to the next, starting at the Visitor Center.

VISITOR CENTER
Start at the Visitor Center for an overview of the site and its various exhibits. As you exit, don't miss the large photograph on the side of the building opposite, depicting this section of the border strip in 1989.

WINDOW OF REMEMBRANCE
This series of windows commemorates the 136 people who lost their lives due to the wall. Its goal—to individualize the victims with photos, names, and birth and death dates—is reinforced by the ever present array of personally placed flowers, stones, and candles.

DEATH STRIP
Drop into the **Documentation Center** for an exhibition on the street's history. Climb to the top of the adjacent **viewing platform** for a physical (and sobering) overview of the site. You'll be looking down, specifically, onto a 230-foot-long section (70 m) of Death Strip, complete with Stasi watchtower.

CHAPEL OF RECONCILIATION
This distinctively round, wooden-slatted chapel was built as a memorial to the original church on

this site, which was dramatically and controversially demolished by the East German government in 1985 to make way for border expansions. At noon on Tuesday through Friday, a prayer service commemorates a different victim of the Berlin Wall.

BORDER HOUSE
A little farther on from the chapel, the exposed remains of a former border house are accompanied by a video on the lives of the residents and some of the escape attempts made. A marked trail highlights **Tunnel 57**—one of the most audacious of the Berlin Wall escapes, in which a 39-foot-long (12 m) tunnel allowed some 57 people to escape in 1964.

BERLIN'S EAST

Bernauer Strasse 111 and 119 • www.berliner-mauer-gedenkstaette.de • 030 21 30 85 123 • Visitor Center closed Mon. • S-Bahn: Nordbahnhof

The Trendy East

Following the collapse of the Berlin Wall, the vast migration from east to west was accompanied by a steady trickle in the other direction as artists and property developers vied for buildings in the city's eastern districts. For a quarter of a century the two groups have waged a battle of the creative over the commercial, of the squat over the penthouse, and it is not over yet.

In its heyday, almost every surface of Kunsthaus Tacheles was painted—inside and out. Opposite: The huge gallery space at Hamburger Bahnhof

The migrants set their sights on areas in Mitte, Prenzlauer Berg, and Friedrichshain, whose proximity to the Berlin Wall—both to the east and to the west—had made them, if not uninhabitable, certainly undesirable. The abundance of cheap and derelict housing in these areas was fertile ground for creative and commercial types. While artists, poets, and punks set up squats, underground nightclubs, and impromptu art galleries in abandoned industrial buildings, property developers embarked on a rigorous program of gentrification.

Battle of the Giants

Today, Berlin's subculture of graffiti and techno-clubbing is legendary. It draws big artists and even bigger crowds and is a major contributor to the city's economy. But the property developers want more of the action. In 2013, **Kunsthaus Tacheles,** a landmark squat in Mitte, was closed down and earmarked for redevelopment. Renowned for its ad hoc bars, alternative vibe, and graffiti-scrawled walls, the building had been at the epicenter of Berlin's hip art scene since the 1990s, when a group of artists rescued it from demolition. Its closure is emblematic of the gentrification process that is affecting the East. In recent years, luxury apartment complexes have sprung up like mushrooms, literally towering over the East Side Gallery, and citizen protests have been of little use. Nevertheless, the east remains a hub of art, design, and fashion—it's just that most of the action is happening in shiny new buildings instead of graffiti-covered squats.

Art Action

With an edgy mix of underground bars and independent galleries, the part of Mitte formerly known as Spandauer Vorstadt—the streets south

MUST-SEE **GALLERIES**

The Sammlung Boros
Berlin's most unique modern art venue is set in a World War II bunker. **Reinhardtstrasse 20, www.sammlung-boros.de, €€€, closed Mon.–Wed. (upon reservation only)**

Hamburger Bahnhof
A permanent collection, plus regular exhibitions from international artists. **Invalidenstrasse 50–51, www.smb.museum, 030 26 64 24 242, €€€, closed Mon.**

Sammlung Hoffmann
An impeccable collection of 20th-century art. **Sophie-Gips-Höfe, Sophienstrasse 21, www.sammlung-hoffmann .de, 030 28 49 91 20, €€€, guided tours on Sat.**

of (and including) Torstrasse that flow between Alte Schönhauser Strasse and Oranienburger Strasse—remains Berlin's primary art hub. **Auguststrasse** is recognized as Berlin's unofficial art mile—so-called for the sheer number of art galleries that line the street. The **KW Institute for Contemporary Art** (*Auguststrasse 69, www.kw-berlin.de, temporarily closed, events and exhibition available online*) is a dedicated space for uncompromising, cutting-edge art. At No. 26 is the **EIGEN + ART gallery** (*www.eigen-art.com, closed Sun.–Mon.*), founded in Leipzig and a key player in Berlin's contemporary scene since the 1990s, featuring well-known artists and young promises in different art media (conceptual, video, installation, and so on).

Fashion Parade

Fashion is a big deal in Berlin. There is no shortage of fashion weeks (in January and July), during which the city seethes with events. The eastern districts have nurtured an army of local designers that includes **Claudia Skoda** (*Alte Schönhauser Strasse 35,*

The Sunday thrift market in RAW-Tempel Gelände

www.claudiaskoda.com, 0176 43 44 25 66). Having started out in the 1970s, Skoda designs exclusive knitwear that remains as au courant around the world as it ever was. More recent appearances on the fashion scene include Alexandra Fischer-Roehler and Johanna Kühl *(Linienstrasse 44, www.kaviargauche.com, closed Mon.)*, whose elegant, feminine **Kaviar Gauche** label, launched in 2005, is famous for wedding gowns. Boutiques that line Alte Schönhauser Strasse and the surrounding streets of Spandauer Vorstadt include **Schwarzhogerzeil** *(Torstrasse 173, www.schwarzhogerzeil.de, 030 28 87 38 68, closed Sun.)*, specializing in top-end clothing and jewelry.

Clubbing at Berghain in Friedrichshain

Club Scene

A major hub for squatters and anarchists during the 1990s, the Friedrichshain neighborhood has all but succumbed to the gentrification trend in recent years. Much of the action is centered on and around Boxhagener Platz, whose surrounding streets are awash with galleries, shops, cafés, and bars. It is also here that clubbers will find the heavyweights of Berlin's nightclub scene. Legendary techno-haunt **Berghain** *(Am Wriezener Bahnhof, www.berghain.berlin, €€€€)* lies on the border with Kreuzberg. The sprawling **RAW-Tempel Gelände** *(Revaler Strasse 99)*, a sustainable urban project created from a former railway depot, also hosts a cluster of clubs. Among these you'll find the techno-electro **Suicide Circus** *(www.suicide-berlin.com, €€, closed Mon.–Tues.)* and **Cassiopeia** *(www.cassiopeia-berlin.de, closed Mon.–Tues.)*, where an eclectic playlist includes everything from grunge and electro, to hip-hop and reggae. With its 1950s former-GDR (DDR) interior, and room for 1,500 guests, **Astra Kulturhaus** *(www.astra-berlin.de)*, within the same complex, regularly hosts spectacular live music events. Also worth a look is the world's smallest disco, **Teledisko**, made out of a disused telephone booth.

Beer Gardens

From spring to late September, Berliners look to the city's laid-back beer gardens to while away an afternoon or evening. Quench your thirst and soak up a little Berlin spirit in one of these leafy retreats. You'll find a good range of beverages beyond beer—as well as traditional rustic snacks.

■ Prater

The Prater complex in Prenzlauer Berg is a Berlin institution dating back to the mid-19th century. There's nothing fancy here—just simple wooden benches and tables shaded by chestnut trees. Self-service kiosks sell a range of snacks, including sausages, soup, pretzels, and salad. Drink like a local and try the Prater Pils. If you want to out yourself as a tourist, ask for a Berliner Weisse, which comes with a shot of green or red syrup.

Kastanienallee 7–9 • www.pratergarten.de • € • Weather permitting open daily • U-Bahn: Eberswalder Strasse

■ Café am Neuen See

Perhaps Berlin's closest take on the Bavarian beer garden, this lakeside venue in the Tiergarten district draws large crowds in summer. Bavarian pretzels and *Leberkäse* (a traditional Bavarian meat loaf) are standard fare, but you can order pizza, too. Arrive early to grab a shady spot. This is a family friendly establishment, with a sandbox for children.

Lichtensteinallee 2 • www.cafeamneuensee.de • 030 25 44 93 21 • €€ • S-Bahn: Tiergarten

■ Schleusenkrug

This Tiergarten favorite overlooks a stretch of Berlin's Landwehrkanal—the canal that runs from Friedrichshain in the east, through Kreuzberg, and on to Tiergarten in the west. Try one of their draft beers, then sit back and watch as canal boats negotiate the lock.

Müller-Breslau-Strasse • www.schleusenkrug.de • 030 31 39 90 9 • €€ • S-Bahn: Tiergarten

■ Golgatha

Head to Kreuzberg's Viktoriapark, where Golgatha caters to all tastes. Less firmly focused on beer than

Visitors to the Tiergarten district take time out at the Schleusenkrug beer garden.

the Prater, the Golgatha is good for breakfasts, coffee, cake in the afternoon, and predinner cocktails. The grill gets going at midday, and the restaurant serves soups and salads, too. There's dancing here on Friday and Saturday evenings.

Via Katzbachstrasse, Dudenstrasse, Kreuzbergstrasse • www.golgatha-berlin.de • 030 78 52 453 • € • Closed Oct.–March • U-Bahn: Platz der Luftbrücke

■ Brauhaus Südstern
Here's a welcome twist: a beer garden with its own brewery. This Kreuzberg spot on the edge of Volkspark Hasenheide is a quiet place to chill. The home-brewed beers are complemented by hearty fare.

Hasenheide 69 • www.brauhaus-suedstern.de • 030 69 00 16 24 • € • U-Bahn: Südstern

■ Luise
A short walk from the **Botanischer Garten** (see p. 161) in Dahlem, this laid-back, family-friendly beer garden serves classic German dishes from an outdoor grill.

Königin-Luise-Strasse 40–42 • www.luise-dahlem.de • 030 84 18 88 0 • € • U-Bahn: Dahlem-Dorf

Schöneberg & Kreuzberg

Each of the districts that make up Berlin's western inner-city neighborhood has its own distinct character. From west to east, the tranquil charm of Schöneberg's beautifully landscaped squares gives way to the laid-back, anything-goes atmosphere of West Kreuzberg, which then explodes into the vibrant and colorful street-life of East Kreuzberg. These characteristics owe much to the area's past. Schöneberg was a hub for left-wing intellectuals during the Weimar years, while many of the Turkish *Gastarbeiters* (guest workers) who helped rebuild and stimulate the city's postwar economy settled in Kreuzberg. Now that inner-city rents have risen, an influx of artists seeking more affordable lifestyles have added a new, bohemian vibe to the neighborhood.

❰ **Kreuzberg is
renowned for its
brightly painted
facades. The words
on the balcony offer
a Turkish "welcome."**

Schöneberg & Kreuzberg

This tour carves a cultural path through the city and explores the ambience of each distinct area as well as the neighborhood's key sights.

❶ Bayerisches Viertel (see p. 142) To explore this quarter, walk south from Schöneberg's elegant Viktoria-Luise-Platz to Bayerischer Platz, wending your way through the sedate residential streets. Head south toward John-F.-Kennedy-Platz.

❷ Rathaus Schöneberg (see pp. 142–143) See where President John F. Kennedy made his historic speech in support of West Berlin. Take the U-Bahn (U4) and change at Bayerischer Platz (U7) to Yorckstrasse.

❸ Viktoriapark (see pp. 143–144) Admire this park's tumbling waterfall and far-reaching views before leaving from its northern side. Walk east toward Bergmannstrasse and into Kreuzberg.

❹ West Kreuzberg (see p. 144) Explore the numerous boutique stores, cafés, and restaurants on and around Bergmannstrasse, then cross the Landwehrkanal at Lindenstrasse.

SCHÖNEBERG & KREUZBERG DISTANCE: 6.5 MILES (10.5 KM)
TIME: APPROX. 8 HOURS U-BAHN START: VIKTORIA-LUISE-PLATZ

5 **Jüdisches Museum** (see pp. 148–149) Daniel Libeskind's zinc-clad building is a fitting setting for the Jewish Museum. Continue a short way north on Lindenstrasse, turning right and then left onto Alte Jakobstrasse.

6 **Berlinische Galerie** (see p. 145) Take a short break in the gallery's convivial café, before viewing works by the city's most significant artists from 1870 to the present. Continue north on Alter Jakobstrasse to Oranienstrasse, then east to Kottbusser Tor.

8 **Kreuzkölln** (see pp. 146–147) Stroll along the Landwehrkanal on Maybachufer and head south to explore trendy Kreuzkölln, before winding up in one of its hip bars for well-deserved refreshment.

7 **Kottbusser Tor** (see p. 146) The area around Kottbusser Tor is electric day and night. Soak up the atmosphere and enjoy some Turkish or Middle Eastern food, then return to the canal on Kottbusser Damm.

Albert Einstein lived in the Bayerisches Viertel from 1918 to 1933.

Bayerisches Viertel

 Viktoria-Luise-Platz lies at the center of Schöneberg's elegant Bavarian Quarter. Developed during the late 19th century, the area became a cultural hub during the Weimar era (see pp. 64–67). Today, the square retains the geometric landscaping of its original design. A number of pathways radiate from a central fountain, and there are colonnades beneath which you can sit and admire the immaculate topiary.

Film director Billy Wilder lived here *(No. 11)* as a young scriptwriter and Albert Einstein lived nearby *(Haberlandstrasse 8)*. Farther south, **Bayerischer Platz** was once home to psychoanalyst-philosopher Erich Fromm *(No. 1)*.

Walking the streets of this neighborhood, you'll notice colorful images on signs attached to lampposts—a loaf of bread here, a walking stick there. Read the text on the reverse to find simplified versions of anti-Semitic laws introduced by the Nazis in the 1930s: "Berlin Jews may only buy provisions from 4–5 p.m." and "Jewish doctors may no longer practice." Known as **Orte des Erinnerns** (Places of Remembrance), the signs—80 of them in total—urge us to reflect on the persecution of Berlin's Jews, some 16,000 of whom lived in this area before the Holocaust.

Between Viktoria-Luise-Platz and Bayerischer Platz • U-Bahn: Viktoria-Luise-Platz

Rathaus Schöneberg

Schöneberg Town Hall was the seat of West Berlin's government from 1948 to 1990. It stands in John-F.-Kennedy-

Platz, so named following the 35th U.S. president's assassination. It was here that John F. Kennedy delivered his *"Ich bin ein Berliner"* ("I am a Berliner") speech on June 26, 1963, indicating U.S. support for West Berlin following the erection of the Berlin Wall. Inside the building, aside from the grand staircases and walkways—mostly reconstructed—you can admire historical paintings, a bust of Friedrich Ebert, Germany's first president, and views from the **clock tower** *(guided tours only),* where a copy of the **Liberty Bell** chimes the time. The United States presented the bell to Berlin in 1950. There is also a permanent exhibition here about Jewish life in the neighborhood. Entitled **"We were neighbors once—biographies of Jewish contemporary witnesses"** *(www.wirwarennachbarn.de, closed Fri.),* the exhibition relates the lives of 160 local Jews from the turn of the 20th century to the aftermath of World War II, tackling a different topic each year, such as women's biographies or resistance acts. On Tuesdays you'll find a nice food market in full swing in John-F.-Kennedy-Platz, while on weekends, it's a popular flea market that attracts locals to the square (see p. 152).

John-F.-Kennedy-Platz •030 90277-0 • U-Bahn: Rathaus Schöneberg

Viktoriapark

3 West Kreuzberg's Viktoriapark is crowned by Friedrich Schinkel's majestic monument commemorating Prussian victory in the War of Liberation against Napoleon. From the monument, an impressive man-made waterfall tumbles 80 feet (24 m) down to street level (summertime only). A couple of small vineyards—one of which produces

The waterfall at Viktoriapark and the monument that gave Kreuzberg its name

around 200 bottles of wine per year—cover the park's southern slopes, and you'll find the seasonal beer garden **Golgatha** (*closed Oct.–March; see pp. 136–137*) in the southwest corner. If you are visiting Berlin in late summer, you'll catch the annual **Kreuzberger Festliche Tage,** a Festive Days Funfair (*last week Aug./first week Sept.*), with a diverse two-week program of events for all.

Viktoriapark • S-Bahn/U-Bahn: Yorckstrasse

GOOD **EATS**

■ **BRLO BRWHOUSE**
Beer love's paradise: brewery (visitable), restaurant, Biergarten. The structure can be dismantled and reassembled anywhere (in fact, in a few years, it will change locations!). **Schöneberger Strasse 16, en.brlo.de, €€**

■ **RENGER-PATZSCH**
A sophisticated wood-paneled dining room, a changing daily menu that includes some new takes on German classics, and great service make this one of Schöneberg's finest dining experiences. **Wartburgstrasse 54, 030 78 42 0 59, €€€**

■ **PAVILLON AM UFER**
This low-key kiosk with canalside tables and chairs runs a simple menu with dishes that change daily—schnitzel and French fries or herb-crusted fish with rice—as well as crisp, hot waffles. **Uferpromenade at Paul-Lincke-Ufer, €**

West Kreuzberg

④ West Kreuzberg, referred to by locals as 61 after its pre-reunification zip code, is more relaxed than its eastern counterpart, SO36 (see p. 146). Lined with lively restaurants, cafés, and trendy boutiques, Bergmannstrasse and its surrounding streets epitomize this laid-back part of the city. Simply stroll through the area and you'll soon succumb to its relaxed ambience. Step into the **Markthalle am Marheinekeplatz** (*Marheinekeplatz 15, www.meine-markthalle.de, 030 50 56 65 36, closed Sun.*) for fresh, high-quality, local foods and produce from all over the world. With a restaurant, cafés, and all manner of food stands, this is an ideal spot to stop for lunch or a snack. Alternatively, head to **Barcomi's Café** (*Bergmannstrasse 21, en.barcomis.de*).

Bergmannstrasse and around • U-Bahn: Gneisenaustrasse

Jüdisches Museum

⑤ See pp. 148–149.

Lindenstrasse 9–14 • www.jmberlin.de • 030 25 99 33 00 • €€ (temporary exhibitions) • Closed Rosh Hashanah, Yom Kippur, Nov. 12, and Dec. 24 • U-Bahn: Kochstrasse

Two stairways crisscross at the center of the lofty main hall at the Berlinische Galerie.

Berlinische Galerie

6 This modern, spacious whitewashed gallery in a former glass warehouse showcases Berlin-made modern art, photography, and architecture. The ground floor is dedicated to temporary exhibitions while, upstairs, a permanent exhibition spans the major German art movements between 1870 and the present day with works by Max Liebermann, Felix Nussbaum, Otto Dix, and George Grosz always on display. Among the more quirky exhibits is **"Pulvarium"** (2005) by Jenny Michel and Michael Hoepfel, a vast collection of dust bunnies, pinned and mounted like butterflies in 40 specimen cases, each one labeled using a system not unlike Carl Linnaeus's binomial nomenclature. The stylish **Café Dix** *(cafe-dix.berlin),* with its modern interior and terrace, is a great place to peruse the program of upcoming exhibitions, screenings, and art classes.

Alte Jakobstrasse 124–128 • www.berlinischegalerie.de • 030 78 90 26 00 • €€ (free first Mon. of the month) • Closed Tues., Dec. 24 and 31 • U-Bahn: Kochstrasse

An early electric kettle designed by Peter Behrens for AEG, on show at the Museum der Dinge

Kottbusser Tor

7 Lively East Kreuzberg, also known as SO36, is grittier than **West Kreuzberg** (see p. 144) and has more of an inner-city buzz. Its hub, Kottbusser Tor, has earned the moniker **Little Istanbul** owing to the high number of Turkish inhabitants renting apartments in the 1950s housing projects that flank the area. Visit on a Tuesday or Friday afternoon and jostle with locals at the Turkish market (see p. 152) that lines **Maybachufer**— the south bank of the Landwehrkanal.

North of Kottbusser Tor, independent stores, cafés, and bars line Oranienstrasse, including the legendary **SO36** (*Oranienstrasse 190, so36.com, 030 61 40 13 06*), a bastion of punk rock and other new wave music since the 1970s. Farther along, the engaging **Museum der Dinge** (Museum of Things; *Oranienstrasse 25, www.museumderdinge.de, 030 92 10 63 11, €€, closed Tues.–Wed.*) traces a history of German design via cabinets of curiosities, from pots and pans to key chains. In summer, nearby Moritzplatz hosts the so-called **Prinzessinnengarten** (*Moritzplatz, prinzessinnengarten-kreuzberg.net, check the website for dates and opening hours*), a community gardening project, where you can relax in a lovely garden café.

Intersection of Skalitzer Strasse and Kottbusser Damm • U-Bahn: Kottbusser Tor

Kreuzkölln

8 Berliners have dubbed the area immediately south of the Landwehrkanal, Kreuzkölln. The name is a mash-up of Kreuzberg to the west and Neukölln to the south. This district exudes a homegrown atmosphere of boho gentrification, thanks to its multitude of fashion boutiques, art spaces, cocktail bars, and interesting combinations of all three, such as **Sing Blackbird** (*Sanderstrasse 11*), where you can buy vintage clothing from the 1970s to the 1990s, eat vegan food on mismatched china in its adjoining café, and sometimes catch an exhibition or a movie.

Farther south is **Weserstrasse**, one of the trendier streets that runs into the Neukölln district, a once gritty working-class neighborhood that is now on the cusp of gentrification. Here Turkish *döner* shops vie with classy wine bars, including **Vin Aqua Vin** (*Weserstrasse 204, www.vinaquavin.de, 030 94 05 28 86*), and café-bars such as **Ä** (*Weserstrasse 40, ae-neukoelln.de, 0177 40 63 837*), whose grungy interior draws a cool-but-casual clientele for concerts, storytelling evenings, and more.

East of Kottbusser Damm • U-Bahn: Schönleinstrasse

Neukölln's Ä bar epitomizes the cool, urban atmosphere of this trendy neighborhood.

Jüdisches Museum

Berlin's Jewish Museum records the horrors of the Holocaust and explores the history of Jewish-German relations before and since.

Libeskind's brutal exterior of the Jewish Museum presents a challenge from the offset.

Designed by renowned American architect Daniel Libeskind, Berlin's Jewish Museum, a defiantly angular building clad in zinc, with violent gashes for windows, forms a dislocated Star of David when seen from above. From the 18th-century Collegienhaus (Old Building), a venue for concerts and events, a black slate gangway leads to the museum's Trio of Axes—three deliberately askew and overlapping corridors that take you on a 2,000-year journey through the history of Jewish people in Germany.

From the Old Building, descend to the museum's Trio of Axes, all of which start in the same place. Below is the recommended order for seeing them.

■ AXIS OF THE HOLOCAUST

Eerily lit display cases contain the poignant possessions of those who died in the Holocaust and accounts of those who escaped it. They include the personal mementos of Leo Scheuer, who eluded the Nazis by hiding in a hole in the ground for 15 months, and the letters of "Aimee and Jaguar"—a lesbian Jewish-German couple who were separated by the Nazis.

■ VOIDED VOID

At the end of the Axis of the Holocaust stands the **Holocaust Tower,** a silo with a tiny slit at the top to admit light and sound. There is a metal ladder on one wall, but it is out of reach. Cold and dark, the space creates a deeply unsettling representation of captivity. Libeskind called this space a voided void. It is one of several empty spaces that extend to the building's full height, glimpsed now and then through slits in the museum walls. Barred to the public, the voids represent the absence of Jews.

■ AXIS OF EXILE

This uneven and gradually narrowing walkway leads outside the main building to the **Garden of Exile**—49 concrete columns erected on a slanting floor. The exhibit represents the alien and unnerving experience of exile.

■ AXIS OF CONTINUITY

This, the longest of the three corridors, winds through the main exhibition on Jewish-German relations through the centuries. The new, interactive layout tells the story of Jewish religion and culture through ritual or everyday objects. The tour is divided into five chapters, with more emphasis given to the post-World War II period. A section is devoted to temporary exhibitions, while a new area for children, called **Anoha,** takes the narrative of Noah's Ark from the Torah as the starting point for a journey into the future.

Lindenstrasse 9–14 • www.jmberlin.de • 030 25 99 33 00 • €€ (for temporary exhibitions) • Closed Rosh Hashanah, Yom Kippur, Nov. 12, and Dec. 24 • U-Bahn: Kochstrasse

City of Diversity

Around 800,000 Berlin residents—more than 20 percent of the population—were not born in Germany. More than 190 countries are represented by these Berliners, most of whom come from Poland, Syria, and Turkey. Walk the streets of central Berlin and German is the lingua franca. Head a little south or east, however, and Turkish or Vietnamese voices are more likely to meet your ears.

**Ghanaian dancers take to the streets in the Karneval der Kulturen festival.
Opposite: Locals sample the Turkish delights at the twice-weekly market on Maybachufer in Kreuzberg.**

Guest Workers

Postwar immigration began in West Germany during the 1950s. The government recruited immigrants in as *Gastarbeiter* (guest workers), not only to compensate for the country's postwar labor shortage, but also to assist with the so-called *Wirtschaftswunder* (Economic Miracle) of the 1960s and 1970s. It was of benefit to the West's Cold War strategy that Germany—being on the East–West border—was seen to be booming, thanks to U.S. Marshall Plan subsidies aimed at rebuilding Europe.

The largest group of immigrants were Turks, who began arriving in October 1961. Initially, the government limited the length of time guest workers could stay in Germany to one year. Other restrictions—relating to housing, education, and family reunion—also applied. Decades passed before workers eventually became permanent residents, settling in Berlin with their families.

Although the Turkish community remains the largest ethnic group in Berlin, a second wave of immigrants swept in from Eastern Europe in the 1980s. Known as *Aussiedler* (resettlers), they comprised ethnic Germans from Romania, Poland, and the collapsing states of the former Soviet Union.

Cultural Legacy

Around 200 different countries are represented in Berlin today—a hodgepodge of non-German communities living side by side in the traditional immigrant districts of Kreuzberg, Tiergarten, Neukölln, and Schöneberg. The streets may be western European architecturally, but many of the storefronts tell a different story, packed as they are with colorful clothing and ethnic foodstuffs. For four days in May, the Karneval der Kulturen (Carnival of Cultures; *www.karneval.berlin*) celebrates the city's diversity with events centered around a parade through the streets of Kreuzberg.

ETHNIC **EATERIES**

Cô Cô-Bánh Mì Deli This tiny Vietnamese restaurant in the Mitte district is popular for its meat- or vegetable-filled baguettes *(banh mi)* **Rosenthaler Strasse 2, www.cocobanhmideli.de, €**

Defne Dine on Turkish classics while overlooking the Landwehrkanal. **Planufer 92c, 030 81 79 71 11, €€**

Maly Ksiaze Polish sweet and savory dumplings *(pierogi)* in the heart of Kreuzberg. **Lillienthalstrasse 6, 030 62 90 80 68, €**

Maroush Traditional Lebanese fare at very reasonable prices. **Adalbertstrasse 93, 030 69 53 61 71, €**

SCHÖNEBERG & KREUZBERG

Street Markets

Almost every neighborhood in Berlin has its own street market selling produce, secondhand furniture, street food, and often all three. Those in the inner-city areas pull in the biggest crowds, and the food stalls on Winterfeldtplatz and Mauerpark's flea market draw foodies and vintage fans from all over town.

■ SCHÖNEBERG
Operating every Saturday since 1990, this weekly market on **Winterfeldtplatz** (*www.winterfeldt-markt.de, 8 a.m.–4 p.m.*) has mushroomed from a couple of stalls to more than 200 today, selling meat, fish, produce, clothes, and flowers. It is now open on Wednesday mornings (*8 a.m.–2 p.m.*) as well. **John-F.-Kennedy-Platz** (see pp. 142–143) hosts a food market on Tuesdays (*8 a.m.–1 p.m.*) and a busy flea market during the weekends (*Sat.–Sun. 8 a.m.–4 p.m.*).

■ KREUZBERG
For an authentic Turkish bazaar vibe, head to the busy market on Landwehrkanal's **Maybachufer** on Tuesday or Friday (*11 a.m.–6:30 p.m.*). **Markthalle Neun** (*Eisenbahnstrasse 42/43, www.markthalleneun.de*) hosts a market of farmers and various food

products (*Tues.–Fri. noon–6 p.m., Sat. 10 a.m.–6 p.m.*), with street food stalls on Thursday evenings (*5–10 p.m.*) and a few food-related events.

■ MITTE
On weekends, Central Mitte holds an arts market between Schlossbrücke and Museumsinsel (*10 a.m.–4 p.m.*) selling books, photographs, and paintings. There is a weekend flea market (*Sat.–Sun., 11 a.m.–5 p.m.*) with around 60 stalls near the Bode-Museum (see sidebar p. 75) farther along the river. A twice-weekly market at **Hackescher Markt** (*Thurs., 9 a.m.–6 p.m., Sat. 10 a.m.–6 p.m.*) sells food, leather goods, jewelry, watches, and arts and crafts.

■ CHARLOTTENBURG
One of the biggest and most famous weekend flea markets in Berlin spreads over sprawling Strasse des 17. Juni

A lively flea market sprawls over the cobblestones in the Mauerpark on Sundays.

(*Sat.–Sun., 10 a.m.–5 p.m.*). Here, you'll find secondhand antiques, vinyl, and an arts market—prices aren't cheap and bargains are rare, but the atmosphere is great.

■ PRENZLAUER BERG

A Thursday organic food market on pretty **Kollwitzplatz** (*noon–7 p.m.*) sells high-end produce from Brandeburg farms—perfect for summer picnics. On Sundays, Berliners flock to the flea market at **Mauerpark** (*Bernauer Strasse 63–64, www.flohmarktimmauerpark.de, 10 a.m.–6 p.m.*) for clothes, records,

and antiques. On Sundays, retro design pieces and vintage furniture, clothes, and shoes are the draw at **Arkonaplatz** (*10 a.m.–4 p.m.*).

■ FRIEDRICHSHAIN

An upbeat crowd throngs to the Saturday food market on **Boxhagener Platz** (*9 a.m.–3:30 p.m.*). Some come specifically for the freshly cooked street food, such as Turkish *gözleme* (savory pastries), grilled fish, and bruschetta. On Sundays, a flea market (*10 a.m.–6 p.m.*) sells the usual assemblage of vinyl, jewelry, books, and vintage curiosities.

Dahlem & the West

Berlin's leafy western suburbs delight and surprise visitors, especially in summer. Just past the borders of Charlottenburg stands the Olympiastadion, the first large-scale architectural project undertaken by the Nazis and a striking symbol of their oppressive power. From the stadium, the vast Grunewald forest stretches south, crossed by walking and cycling trails and lapped by the Grunewaldsee. On the shore of the lake, Jagdschloss Grunewald, a 16th-century hunting lodge, displays paintings by masters of the German Renaissance. Just to the west of here are the watery attractions of the Havel River and the popular Wannsee area with its island and beaches, while to the east, sleepy Dahlem offers an excellent museum, Saturday markets, and world-class botanical gardens.

◐ **Yachts and kayaks
glide through the
water with idyllic
views across the
Grunewaldsee.**

Dahlem & the West

*Reminders of Berlin's checkered past combine with a world-class museum
and botanical gardens on this walk on the west side.*

5 Museum Europäischer Kulturen (see pp. 162–163) Complete your tour browsing several thousand years of history at this purpose-built museum complex.

4 Botanischer Garten (see p. 161) Explore Berlin's botanical gardens, with landscaped Italian gardens, 19th-century greenhouses, and an arboretum. Retrace your steps on Königin-Luise-Strasse.

1 Olympiastadion (see pp. 158–159) Built by the Nazis for the 1936 Olympics, this stadium is now used for sports events and concerts. Stroll the grounds or join a tour. Take the U-Bahn to Oskar-Helene-Heim, then walk 1 mile (2 km) north.

2 Jagdschloss Grunewald (see p. 159) Now an art gallery, this 16th-century lakeside palace contains German and Dutch paintings and hunting-related paraphernalia. A 20-minute stroll through the forest will bring you to the AlliiertenMuseum.

3 AlliiertenMuseum

(see pp. 160–161) The former library and cinema of the Allied Powers documents the Cold War era. Exhibits include a plane used in the Berlin Airlift and a segment of the Allied spy tunnel. On leaving head north on Clayallee, then east on Königin-Luise-Strasse, passing by the Museum Europäischer Kulturen

Map labels

WILMERSDORF

HALENSEE

Teufelsberg 115 m ▲

Havel

HAVELCHAUSSEE

GRUNEWALD

Grosser Wannsee

WANNSEE

Krumme Lanke

Schlachtensee

PAUL-ERNST-PARK

NIKOLASSEE

Wannsee

Nikolassee

Schlachtensee

Mexikoplatz

Krumme Lanke

Onkel Toms Hütte

Zehlendorf

ZEHLENDORF

DÜPPEL

Sundgauer Strasse

Lichterfelde West

Botanischer Garten

Oskar-Helene-Heim

Dahlem-Dorf

PACELLIALLEE

DAHLEM

SCHMARGENDORF

Breitenbachplatz

Podbielskiallee

Heidelberger Platz

Halensee

Westkreuz

MASUREN ALLEE

...FFÉ-STR.

MesseSüd

Grunewald

MesseNord

KOENIGSALLEE

HAGENSTR.

GRUNEWALD

Grunewaldsee

PÜCKLER-STRASSE

CLAYALLEE

HOHENZOLLERNDAMM

Hohenzollerndamm

HÜTTEN WEG

ONKEL- TOM- STR.

ARGENTINISCHE ALLEE

CLAYALLEE

2 Jagdschloss Grunewald

3 AlliiertenMuseum

4 Botanischer Garten

5 Museum Europäischer Kulturen

0 1 mile

0 2 kilometers

DAHLEM & THE WEST DISTANCE: 7.75 MILES (12.5 KM) TIME: APPROX. 6.5 HOURS S-BAHN/U-BAHN START: OLYMPIASTADION

U.S. sprinter Jesse Owens (right) storms to the finish line at the Berlin Olympics in 1936.

Olympiastadion

1 The 75,000-capacity Olympic Stadium, home to local soccer heroes Hertha BSC since 1963, has successfully hosted two FIFA World Cup competitions as well as pop luminaries, including the Rolling Stones and Madonna. Designed by the Nazis for the 1936 Olympics, the neoclassical structure—which survived the war almost intact—was modeled on Rome's Colosseum. The Nazis saw the Olympics as a chance to display Aryan superiority, a strategy that was undermined when African American sprinter Jesse Owens won four gold medals, including the 100-meter dash. You can tour the stadium and its grounds (*from 9 a. m.*), on your own or with a guided tour (*in German and English, more options available*); in the former case it is worth investing in a multimedia guide (€2), which gives 75 to 100 minutes' worth of historical and architectural information about the venue.

Creating an imposing first impression on the east side of the stadium, the vast **Olympischer Platz** leads to two original stone pillars strung with the Olympic rings. Inside, a paved walkway circles the stadium, punctuated with engraved stone columns, 1930s statuary, and the Olympic Bell, complete with Nazi insignia. The bell originally sat inside the 250-foot-high (76 m) **Glockenturm** (bell tower). Climb the tower *(www.glockenturm.de, opening hours vary—check the website before visiting)* for views over Berlin's western suburbs and Grunewald. The stadium's swimming pool is open to the public in summer, when the **Waldbühne** *(www.waldbuehne-berlin.de)*, an open-air stage in Olympiapark, also hosts concerts (see p. 170).

(see p. 170)

Olympischer Platz 3 • olympiastadion.berlin • 030 306 88 888 • €€–€€€€
• S-Bahn/U-Bahn: Olympiastadion

SAVVY TRAVELER

Check venue websites for seasonal opening times (in winter, some sites may only open on weekends). Be sure to start early at Olympiastadion in order to get the most from each site.

Jagdschloss Grunewald

2 Sitting beside the forest-fringed waters of the Grunewaldsee, this 16th-century hunting lodge is the oldest of the many palaces, residences, and parks built in Berlin by the Hohenzollern dynasty. You can access the lodge—now an art gallery—via a leafy forest path popular with joggers, strollers, and dog-walkers. The **Great Hall** displays hunt-related artifacts: a tapestry from around 1700, hunting trophies and paintings, a double-barreled gun from 1550. Upstairs, Dutch and German paintings include nearly 30 by Lucas Cranach the Elder (1472– 1553) and Younger (1515–1586). Stop for coffee and cake in the courtyard or take a stroll beside the lake.

Hüttenweg 100 • www.spsg.de • 0331 96 94 200
• € • Closed Mon. year-round , and Tues.–Fri. Nov.–March • U-Bahn: Oskar-Helene-Heim

A statue of hunting dogs attacking a wild boar outside Jagdschloss Grunewald

AlliiertenMuseum

3 It is impossible to miss the Allied Museum, thanks to the **Hastings TG 503 aircraft** at the entrance. The British plane was one of several hundred used to drop essential supplies into West Berlin during the Soviet blockade of the Allied sectors (see p. 165): at the peak of the airlift, one plane per minute touched down in Berlin. You can currently visit this unique aircraft *(closed Mon., 10 a.m.–6 p.m.)* also from the inside, except during inclement weather or restoration work.

The Allied Museum tells the story of the Western powers in Berlin during the postwar years until the reunification of the city in 1990. The two buildings on either side of the plane originally housed the **Outpost Theater** (cinema) and the Nicholson Memorial Library of the U.S. garrison. An exhibition in the former cinema focuses on the occupation of Berlin by the Allied troops, the airlift, and everyday life in the American, British, and French sectors. It includes a segment

The story of the Allied occupation of Berlin as told through exhibits at the AlliiertenMuseum

of the **spy tunnel** built by American and British intelligence services to tap the telephone lines of the Soviets. Exhibits in the former library focus on military confrontations between East and West during the Cold War. Outside the museum, you can climb aboard a railroad car from the French military train and enter the original guardhouse of **Checkpoint Charlie** (see p. 57).

Clayallee 135 • www.alliiertenmuseum.de • 030 81 81 990 • Closed Mon. • U-Bahn: Oskar-Helene-Heim

Botanischer Garten

4 Lose yourself for an hour or so in the verdant oases of Berlin's Botanical Garden—a whopping 106 acres (43 ha) with around 22,000 plant species. At the southern end, native woody plants and roses stock the arboretum, while to the north are the **Gewächshäuser**—an impressive group of glass and steel greenhouses. The largest has waterfalls and towering bamboo inside. Pick up a map at the entrance or, better still, one of four seasonal leaflets listing 12 blooms to discover on a dedicated trail.

The neighboring **Botanisches Museum** (*temporarily closed, reopening scheduled in 2023*) offers a chance to test and expand your knowledge via dioramas and magnified details of plant structures.

Königin-Luise-Strasse 6–8 • www.bgbm.org • 030 83 85 0100 • Closed Dec. 24 • €€ • U-Bahn: Dahlem-Dorf

Museum Europäischer Kulturen

5 See pp. 162–163.

Arnimallee 25 • www.smb.museum • 030 26 64 24 242 • Closed Mon. • €€ • U-Bahn: Dahlem-Dorf

GOOD **EATS**

■ **CHALET SUISSE**
This restaurant in Grunewald serves French-Swiss dishes, including some game, in a relaxed, semirural setting. **Clayallee 99, 030 83 26 362, €€**

■ **DOMÄNE DAHLEM**
The farm shop in this 800-year-old working farm and open-air agrarian museum sells soups, cakes, sausages, and drinks, which can be eaten on one of the nearby picnic tables. **Königin-Luise-Strasse 49, 030 66 63 000, €**

■ **LUISE**
This elegant space serves draft beers, homemade burgers, and German specialties. There is also a beer garden, a children's playground, and an outdoor grill. **Königin-Luise-Strasse 40–42, 030 84 18 880, €€**

DAHLEM & THE WEST

Museum Europäischer Kulturen

Folklore from Germany and other parts of Europe is on display through a boundless collection of artifacts.

A detail of the large Weihnachtsberg, with scenes from the life of Jesus

The Museum of European Cultures' new exhibition brings together the collections of multiple institutions engaged in the preservation of German anthropological heritage. This museum goes beyond the setting of a traditional ethnographic collection and embraces various aspects of living in a society, by illustrating its shared values and identities. In particular, it focuses on the complex dynamics of the European continent through objects and artifacts from the 18th century onward that tell more than just their use.

Since the transfer of the Asian art and ethnology collections to the **Humboldt Forum** (see pp. 76–77), the former Museen Dahlem complex has concentrated in this single building a coherent itinerary through daily life and cultural contacts between different human groups in Germany and Europe.

■ PERMANENT EXHIBITION

The museum investigates the characteristics of German and European folk cultures, the affinities that exist between them, and the meaning they take on in a context of shared knowledge and coexistence. In this way, each artifact becomes a cue for reflecting on multiple themes, such as the **black Venetian gondola** from 1910, which evokes travel, trade, and local crafts. Another museum attraction is the so-called **Weihnachtsberg** (Nativity Mountain), a 39-foot-long (12 m) model from the Erzgebirge region of eastern Germany that consists of 328 finely crafted figurines depicting episodes from the life of Christ, many of them mechanically operated. Children are always captivated by this huge "nativity scene."

■ NATURE

One section is devoted to the relationship between man and nature, its "cultural" use and pollution, remarking the strong connection that still ties our past to our current issues.

■ A PLACE WHERE THINGS HAPPEN

Events are another important part of the Museum of European Cultures' activities. In the summer, for example, the **Days of European Cultures** are held, dedicated to a different area each year and in collaboration with local associations. Meetings and fairs are also held here, dedicated to textiles and weaving, an area of which the museum can boast valuable pieces. Check the calendar on the website so you don't miss the **Handmade Arts Expo,** created together with French artist Natacha Wolters, and **Textiltag**.

DAHLEM & THE WEST

Arnimallee 25 • www.smb.museum • 030 26 64 24 242 • Closed Mon. • €€ • U-Bahn: Dahlem-Dorf

A Divided City

For four decades of the 20th century, Berlin symbolized a divided Europe. Split politically into East and West following World War II, the city was physically divided by a wall from 1961 until 1989. All but fragments of the Berlin Wall have gone now, but a legacy of division lives on among the city's inhabitants, some of whom look back with nostalgia to former times.

This emblem of a tank decorates a wall at the Soviet war memorial in Schönholzer Heide in former East Berlin. Opposite: A plane brings in much-needed supplies during the Berlin Airlift (1948–1949).

The End of World War II

When Germany capitulated to the Allies in May 1945, Soviet troops took control of Berlin. The victorious Allies met at Cecilienhof Palace in Potsdam in July to sketch out a new European order. They divided Germany into four zones (U.S., British, French, and Soviet). The capital, Berlin, was in the Soviet sector, but it, too, was split into four zones in what was to be a temporary military occupation.

One City: Four Zones

The Allies planned for a united Germany but could not come to a concrete arrangement with the Soviets. Frustrated by the lack of progress, the U.S., with some support from France and Britain, pressed ahead with economic reforms in West Berlin. In June 1948, the three Western Allies went a step further by introducing a new currency for West Germany and West Berlin without consulting their Soviet partner.

By now it was clear that most Germans did not want to live under a communist system. Crucially, most felt great hostility toward their Soviet occupiers.

This was not just a legacy of Nazi propaganda. Soviet soldiers had raped, and sometimes murdered, thousands of women when they arrived in Berlin—in revenge for the similar atrocities committed by Nazi soldiers in the Soviet Union.

The Berlin Airlift

Moscow reacted with indignation to the currency reforms and imposed a blockade on overland routes connecting West Berlin with the Western Allies' occupied territory in western Germany. For 15 months from June 24, 1948, to May 12, 1949, West Berlin relied for its supplies on air convoys from the West to Tempelhof airport—a memorial to the event stands outside the terminal building. The story is also recounted (mainly from a U.S. perspective) at the **AlliiertenMuseum** (see pp. 160–161).

REMEMBERING
THE WALL

Several initiatives around Berlin recall life in the divided city. For an impressive and neutral narrative, head for the **Gedenkstätte Berliner Mauer** (see pp. 130–131). Stretching along Bernauer Strasse, running northeast of Nordbahnhof, the memorial includes a stretch of the former wall, a museum, and a beautiful chapel. An exhibition at the **Tränenpalast** (Reichstagufer 17, www.hdg.de, 030 46 77 77 911) near Friedrichstrasse S-Bahn station recalls the leave-taking and tears that were once part of everyday life at this former crossing point between the two halves of Berlin.

DAHLEM & THE WEST

The building of the wall left the 18th-century Brandenburg Gate marooned in East Germany, visible from the West but unreachable. When the wall came down in 1989 (opposite), the gate featured in many images of liberation.

Two German States

The Western Allies' decision in early 1949 to set up a separate country on their territory—the Federal Republic of Germany, known as West Germany, with a parliament in Bonn—further provoked the Soviet Union. West Berlin was never part of West Germany, but the enclave sent observers to the Bonn parliament. The Soviets, in turn, set up the German Democratic Republic in the east in October 1949.

The Building of the Wall

Arrangements for transit between East and West Berlin existed through the 1950s. Many Berliners lived in one half of the city but worked in the other. This made Berlin the focus of mass emigration from the east, with at least a quarter of the East German population voting with their feet.

In 1961, the East Germans built the Berlin Wall, severing almost all connections between the two halves of Berlin. It was understandable that the communist government wanted to stop the exodus, but as a symbol of their regime it was a propaganda catastrophe. Photographs of East Germans trying to flee across the barrier appeared in the Western media, contributing to the negative image of the communist regime, especially when those fleeing were shot dead.

The End of an Era

In the late 1980s, demonstrations in East German cities spurred the debate about change in the communist East. The Soviet Union took the lead in defusing Cold War tensions, and Mikhail Gorbachev's visit to Berlin on October 7, 1989, signaled this willingness to change. Ten days later veteran East German leader Erich Honecker resigned, and on November 9, 1989, the East German government announced the immediate opening of border crossings to the West. A year later, the two German states formally merged.

Legacy of the Wall

Few mourned the disappearance of the wall, but there are some in the east who regret losing the security and stability that came with a socialist society. In many ways, Berlin remains divided. The eastern half of the city still tends to vote for left-leaning political parties, and *solyanka* (a spicy soup) and other Russian dishes still feature on menus in the east. Some older West Berliners look back with affection to a time when Berlin was a western outpost behind the Iron Curtain. Berlin was quieter in those days—and hugely subsidized by the West. Yet it was not just a place for the privileged. Not having any military service, it was also a magnet for freethinkers and liberals. Their communes have almost disappeared as a unified Berlin asserts its status as a world city.

Summer in the City

In summer, Berlin really comes into its own. Cafés and bars spill out onto the sidewalks, and the buzz of endless parties and events, from street festivals to outdoor movies, fills the air. Rivers and lakes offer swimming and boating, and the city's parks provide plenty of spots to throw down a picnic blanket.

DAHLEM & THE WEST

■ SWIMMING

Just west of Dahlem, and a world apart from Berlin's culture-swamped and often gritty inner-city, Wannsee is an idyllic summer playground. Its most obvious warm-weather attraction is the **Strandbad Wannsee** (Wannsee Beach; *Wannseebadweg*), one of Europe's largest and oldest outdoor lidos. An impressive sandy beach lined by rows of classic sausage, beer, and ice-cream stalls and dotted with wicker beach chairs stretches for more than a mile (1.6 km). You can either look for a place on the free beach or reserve your own spot (*www.berlinerbaeder.de*).

To swim in an outdoor pool head straight to **Sommerbad Kreuzberg** (*Prinzenstrasse 113–119, www.berlinerbaeder.de, €€, open June–mid-Sept.*), which has three swimming pools (one of which is unheated and chlorine-free), a large sunbathing area, and access to nearby Böcklerpark.

■ BEACH BARS

Even in the center of Berlin, you will find a surprising number of summer "beach bars" where you can feel sand beneath your feet, sit under a palm tree, and sometimes even swim or play volleyball. The season traditionally starts around Easter and lasts as long as the sun keeps shining—often well into September. Recline in a deck chair, cocktail in hand, and watch the boats go by at **Capital Beach Bar** (*Ludwig-Erhard-Ufer*), between the Reichstag and the Hauptbahnhof. Or head to **Strandbar Mitte** (*Monbijoustrasse 3b*), overlooking the Bode-Museum, where you can loll around in two-seater beach chairs (*Strandkörb*) or play volleyball. If you're traveling with children, they'll love the children's beach in **Monbijoupark** (*Oranienburger Strasse 78, 030 22 19 00 11*). There is lawn space for adults, an ice-cream kiosk, and a small playground.

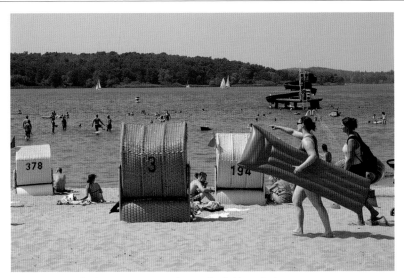
The lido at Strandbad Wannsee attracts thousands of visitors during summer.

■ SUMMER FESTIVALS

During Pentecost (late May/early June), Kreuzberg comes alive with the **Karneval der Kulturen** (*www.karneval.berlin*), a street festival celebrating the cultural diversity of Berlin with music, food, floats, and a grand parade. The carnival starts on Hermannplatz and continues to Möckernstrasse. It is an event that draws more than one million people.

For about three weeks at the turn of July and August, the **Deutsch-Amerikanisches Volksfest** (German-American Peoples Festival; *www. deutschamerikanischesvolksfest.de*) has become an institution in the city: you'll find everything from fairground-style rides like roller coasters, bumper cars, and carousels to custom-made ghost towns. Expect plenty of food and drink stalls serving up U.S.-style cuisine including good old-fashioned hot dogs and hamburgers. Leaving its historic location in the Zehlendorf district, the festival moved for a few years to Mitte and then to Marienpark, but it is not yet certain where the next editions will be held.

For three days at the beginning of August, Berlin's east hosts the **Internationales Berliner Bierfestival**

Club der Visionäre on the Spree River

come here to enjoy a nighttime movie with a bottle of wine and a picnic. You'll find a program of international movies, including some from February's **Berlinale** (see p. 102). A number of films are screened in English with German subtitles (you can find the program and locations in Kreuzberg and Wedding on the website).

■ MUSIC EVENTS

At the end of June and for one night only, the **Waldbühne** (*Am Glockenturm, www.waldbuehne -berlin.de, 01806 57 00 70, €€€€€*), a beautiful outdoor amphitheater in the woods at Dahlem, plays host to the **Berliner Philharmonie** for a themed festival of sounds that can range from Latin American rhythms to Tchaikovsky. It marks the end of the philharmonic's annual program.

In Kreuzberg, there is little to rival the charm of the canalside **Club der Visionäre** (*Am Flutgraben 2, www .clubdervisionaere.com, 030 532 151 43, €€*). Open year-round, this music venue comes into its own in summer. Listen to the club's evening program sitting beneath a huge weeping willow that overhangs waterfront decking.

A very different venue, for a few days each summer, Berlin's handsome Gendarmenmarkt near Unter den

(International Beer Festival; *www .internationales-berliner-bierfestival.de*), drawing around 800,000 visitors from all over the world. Known as both the "beer mile" and the "longest beer garden in the world," the event showcases around 350 breweries from 90 countries. Take your pick from around 2,400 beer specialties.

■ OPEN-AIR CINEMA

A great way to spend an evening under the stars is to attend the **Freiluftkino** (Open-air Cinema; *www.freiluftkino -berlin.de, €€, May–Sept.*) in **Volkspark Friedrichshain** (see p. 128). Berliners

DAHLEM & THE WEST

Linden is transformed by **Classic Open Air** *(www.classicopenair.de, 030 31 57 54 13, €€€€€, early July)*, a series of music events ranging from opera and operetta to pop, soul, and jazz.

In Berlin's east is **Mauerpark** *(Gleimstrasse 55, www.bearpitkaraoke .com)*, part of the so-called Death Strip that ran alongside the former Berlin Wall (the name means "wall park"). It is one of the district's most popular hangouts in summer, when lively karaoke sessions take place in the amphitheater, weather permitting *(Sun., Apr.–Oct., 3 p.m.)*.

■ LANGE NACHT DER MUSEEN

The annual **Long Night of Museums** *(www.lange-nacht-der-museen.de, last Sat. of Aug.)* involves some 80 museums staying open way beyond their usual closing times. You'll have the opportunity to take a closer look at paintings, sculptures, and installations and watch a number of specially produced art performances, guided tours, and concerts. There are shuttle buses operating overnight that travel between the institutions involved, while the museum ticket entitles you to free travel on public transportation.

The Bearpit Karaoke sessions in Mauerpark are open to all aspiring stars of the stage.

PART 3

Travel Essentials

PLANNING YOUR TRIP

When to Go
Try as you will, there's no bad time to visit Berlin. The warm seasons are the obvious favorites for exploring the city on foot—spring, summer, and early fall. That said, the colder months offer many of the same world-class attractions.

To avoid the biggest crowds, enjoy a festival, and have a shot at decent weather, try visiting in the spring shoulder season from **April through early June,** or in the fall from **September to October.** Berlin's hectic pace slows a beat, hotels are cheaper, and lines shrink at the popular museums.

In the high-season months of **July and August,** Berlin crawls with tourists but on the upside, reliably balmy temperatures, beach bars, and a multitude of outdoor events will keep you smiling. In **December,** the Christmas markets spread a special magic, and some say you haven't lived until you pop the bubbly on New Year's Eve at the Brandenburg Gate.

Climate
Berlin's relatively cool, temperate climate has more in common with Moscow than Paris. Seasons are more extreme than the German average, with hot summers and fairly harsh winters. Cold fronts roll in from central Russia, bringing freezing temperatures

and moderate, but usually not paralyzing, amounts of snow. In summer from June to late August, the mercury can soar into the low 90s°F (low 30s°C). Indian summer into late October can be delightful, with blue skies, fluffy clouds, and trees turning to gold.

Insurance
Take out enough travel insurance to cover emergency medical treatment, loss or theft, and repatriation.

Passports
U.S. and Canadian citizens can stay in Germany for up to three months with just a valid passport. No visa is required.

HOW TO GET TO BERLIN

By Airplane
There are surprisingly few direct flights to Berlin from outside Europe. Most arrivals are routed through larger European hubs in London, Amsterdam, or Frankfurt to board a connecting flight.

Since its opening in 2020, only **Berlin Brandenburg Airport (BER)**, named after GDR Chancellor and Nobel Peace Prize winner Willy Brandt, has been in operation. Tegel has ceased operations, while Schönefeld has become Terminal 5 of the new state-of-the-art hub. Terminals 1 and 2 are adjacent to each other (and form a single destination for transportation), while 5 is

farther away and cannot be reached on foot.

For details of connections, contact the flight information desk *(030 60 91 60 910)* or see the full schedule on the airport website *(ber.berlin-airport.de).*

The train station is located below Terminal 1, and regional trains, the Airport Express, and the S-Bahn (S5 and S45, which also connect to Terminal 5) arrive there. By bus, all terminals can be reached by express lines X7 and X71, to be taken at the Rudow terminus of the U-Bahn (U7); alternatively, you can travel on city lines 163, 164, 171, 744. The airport is included in Berlin Transport Zone C *(single trip €3.60);* you pay extra on shuttles. A cab ride to Mitte costs about €50 and takes more or less 30 minutes.

By Train
Germany's efficient national railway network is run by **Deutsche Bahn** (DB; *www.bahn.de*). Long-distance IntercityExpress (ICE), InterCity (IC), and EuroCity (EC) trains stop at both the main Hauptbahnhof and Ostbahnhof stations. Regional-Express (RE) and Interregio-Express (IRE) trains link Berlin to centers in the surrounding state of Brandenburg and beyond. Every large station has a **Reisezentrum** (travel service center) with timetables and connections posted in the main hall. Train tickets are available at the service center, from DB vending machines,

or online. Only on ICE and EC trains, you can buy the ticket on board with a € 17 surcharge. Foreign visitors are eligible for special vacation passes.

By Bus

Slow but tolerably comfortable long-distance buses link Berlin to the rest of Europe. Most arrive at the ZOB (Zentraler Omnibusbahnhof Berlin; *zob.berlin*), the central bus station in Charlottenburg opposite the Funkturm (radio tower).

GETTING AROUND

Public Transportation

Berlin's tightly woven network of buses, trams (Strassenbahn), subways (U-Bahn), and commuter rail (S-Bahn) is run by the **Berlin Transport Authority BVG** (*www.bvg.de, 030 19 449*). U- and S-Bahns run from around 4:30 a.m. until 1:30 a.m., when night buses take over. On Fridays and Saturdays, U- and S-Bahns run all night.

Combined tickets are valid on buses, trams, and commuter rail. Buy tickets from ticket machines at U- or S-Bahn stops or, in the case of buses and trams, from the conductor or onboard ticket machine. Validate your ticket before traveling in a time-stamping machine—found inside buses and trams and on the station platforms. Failure to do so may incur a fine.

Berlin is divided into three public transportation zones: A and B for the central area, and C for outer districts, including Potsdam and Berlin Brandeburg Airport. Most destinations in town can be reached with an A-plus-B ticket.

Various tourist cards are available at ticket offices and many Berlin hotels. They include the **Berlin WelcomeCard,** which offers great flexibility and discounts of up to 50% at about 180 partner establishments: You can choose the areas of the city in which to travel for free by public transport, the number of days and, if necessary, the supplement to visit the Museumsinsel museums for free (*www.berlin-welcomecard.de; from €24 for 48 hours bands A and B to €55 for 72 hours with Museumsinsel and band C supplement*). The **Museum Pass Berlin,** on the other hand, provides free admission for 3 days to 30 institutions, including the Museumsinsel (*www.visitberlin.de; from €29*). A very useful smartphone resource are the official BVG apps Fahrinfo-App and Jelbi-App, with all the mobility options and a route calculator.

By Bicycle

Berlin's growing network of bike paths is a serious alternative to road transportation and arguably the most pleasant and convenient way to get around.

The city has hundreds of miles of routes snaking through town and out into the countryside. A route map published by German cycling association **ADFC** (*www.adfc.de, 030 448 47 24*) is a good investment. You can plan urban journeys online at **BBBike** (*www.bbbike.de*), allowing you to set preferences for road type, greenery, and traffic lights.

You can take your bike on long-distance trains by reserving a stall and paying a special fare. Board carriages marked with the bike symbol. On S-Bahn and U-Bahn trains, you can board with your bike by paying an extra fee.

A reliable bicycle agency is **Fat Tire** (under the Fernsehturm/TV Tower; *www.berlinfahrradverleih.com, 030 24 04 79 91*).

Operated by DB, **Call a Bike** (*www.callabike.de*) is a bike sharing service operating in 50 German cities; in Berlin there are 350 stations where bikes can be picked up and delivered via smartphone apps.

By Taxi

Taxi stands are located at airports, at train and subway stations, and throughout the city, but you can also hail taxis in the street. Flag fall is €3.90, then €2.30 per km for the first 7 kilometers, then €1.65 per km after that. A tip for nightclubbers: A Kurzstrecke (short trip) up to 2 km (1.2 miles) costs €6—inform the driver you want this fare before you set off.

By Train

For excursions farther afield, you'll need to take regional or national trains run by **Deutsche Bahn** (*www.bahn.de*).

PRACTICAL ADVICE

Electricity

German circuits (mostly) use 220 volts. American appliances need adaptor plugs, and those that operate on 110 volts will also need a transformer.

Money Matters

The currency of Germany is the euro (€). There are 100 cents to 1 euro. Euro banknotes come in denominations of 5, 10, 20, 50, and 100, as well as the rare 200 and 500 bills. Coins come in €1 and €2 as well as 1, 2, 5, 10, 20, and 50 cents.

Most major banks have ATMs for bank cards and credit cards with instructions in several languages. Cash and traveler's checks can be exchanged in banks and currency booths at railroad stations and airports.

Opening Times

■ Banks: 8 a.m.–4 p.m. (around 5:30 p.m. on Thurs.); some in outlying areas close for lunch between 1 p.m. and 2 p.m. Closed Saturday and Sunday.
■ Museums: Generally 9 a.m–6 p.m. Many museums are closed on Monday but stay open late on Thursday evenings.
■ Pharmacies: Open during normal store hours and on a rotation schedule to cover nights and weekends.
■ Retailers: Weekdays 8:30 a.m.–6:30 p.m. (until 8 p.m. or 10 p.m. for many department stores and on Thursdays). On Saturday, hours are 8:30 a.m.–

8 p.m., although smaller shops close between noon and 2 p.m. Stores are generally closed on Sunday, except in airports and large train stations.

Post Offices

Post offices run by Deutsche Post, the national mail service, run like clockwork but are few and far between. Opening hours are generally 8 a.m. to 6 p.m. Monday to Friday and until noon on Saturday. Branches in airports and larger train stations are open seven days a week. Buy stamps at the post office counter or from vending machines outside. To find a post office branch near you, go to *www.deutschepost.de* and click on "Filiale finden."

Telephones

Public telephones are available in ever dwindling numbers. The rate from telephone booths run by national provider Deutsche Telekom is about 23 cents a minute. Most public telephones are card operated, although some also take coins. Phone cards (*Telefonkarten*) are sold at post offices, convenience stores, and supermarkets for €10, €15, and €20. Note that numbers prefixed with 0900, 0180, or 0190 are toll numbers.

If you bring your cell phone to Germany, make sure it is compatible with Europe's GSM network. To keep costs down, sign up for an international roaming plan with your mobile provider. Or, once in Berlin you can a buy a

local SIM card or inexpensive mobile with prepaid airtime. Check the offers at electronics warehouses like MediaMarkt or Saturn on Alexanderplatz.

Time Differences

Germany is on Central European Time (CET), six hours ahead of Eastern Standard Time. Noon in Germany is 6 a.m. in New York. Clocks move ahead one hour in the summer.

Travelers With Disabilities

There are access ramps and elevators in many public buildings, including train stations, museums, and theaters. Most buses and trams carry a blue wheelchair symbol and have special ramps. Most S- and U-Bahn stations downtown have ramps or elevators; exactly which ones do is displayed on the BVG network map. For information and support, contact the **Berlin Disabled Association** (*Jägerstrasse 63d, www.bbv-ev.de, 030 20 43 847*).

VISITOR INFORMATION

The city's tourist authority, **Berlin Tourismus & Kongress** (BTM; *www.visitberlin.de, 030 25 00 23 33*), is helpful and well organized. A large Infostore is located in the Hauptbahnhof (8 a.m.–8 p.m. daily, entrance on Europaplatz). You'll find branches in the south wing of the Brandenburg Gate, at the Park Inn hotel at Alexanderplatz, and at airports. The official **About Berlin app** provides information on more than 200 sights; it is free and also works offline.

EMERGENCIES

Crime & Police
Berlin is a remarkably safe place, and big-city common sense will steer you clear of most trouble. Some U- and S-Bahn stations in parts of Kreuzberg and Friedrichshain—Kottbusser Tor, Görlitzer Bahnhof, and Warschauer Strasse, for instance—may look rough, but the hang-abouts are generally harmless and looking for handouts. More care is urged in the outer suburbs of Lichtenberg, Marzahn, Neukölln, and Wedding, where muggings and street assaults do sometimes occur.

If you need help for any reason, dial emergency number 110 to contact the police. There are police stations in every district, including the one at Friesenstrasse 16, between Kreuzberg and Tempelhof, and the one at Wedekindstrasse 10, just a 10-minute walk from Ostbahnhof station. The police will take a statement, cancel your credit cards, let you use the telephone, and help contact your embassy. If you encounter trouble on trains, the Bahnpolizei have offices at major stations.

German police officers can be identified by their solid blue uniforms (marked POLIZEI on the back) and blue-and-silver squad cars. Motorized police known as the Verkehrspolizei patrol the streets, roads, and motorways. Many German police officers speak English.

It is the law to carry proof of identification, such as a passport, driver's license, or ID card, with you at all times.

Embassies & Consulates
■ **British Embassy,** Wilhelmstrasse 70–71, www.ukingermany.fco.gov.uk, 030 20 45 70
■ **Canadian Embassy,** Leipziger Platz 17, 030 20 31 20
■ **U.S. Embassy,** American Citizen Services Section, Clayallee 170, de.usembassy.gov, 030 83 05 0

Emergency Phone Numbers
■ Fire department & ambulance (Feuerwehr) 112
■ Police (Polizeinotruf) 110
■ Medical emergency (Notarzt, for house calls) 11 61 17
■ Dental emergency 030 89 00 43 33

Health
Apart from party fatigue, there are few health risks involved in visiting Berlin. For minor ailments, qualified staff at pharmacies offer expert advice. Doctors' consulting hours are normally 9 a.m. to noon and 3 to 6 p.m., except weekends. For urgent attention outside consulting hours, go to a hospital (Krankenhaus). German medical treatment and facilities are generally very good. The **Charité Hospital** has three emergency room locations; the one in Mitte is at Philippstrasse 10 (030 450 531 000).

Lost Property
Your travel insurance should cover the loss or theft of your property if you are not already covered by your home insurance. Theft must be reported to the police so you can obtain a certificate confirming that the crime has been reported. The national rail service, Deutsche Bahn, has its own lost property office (0900 19 90 599), as does the Berlin urban transportation network BVG (030 19 449). For items lost elsewhere, try the Berlin State Central Lost and Found Office (030 90 27 73 101).

Lost/Stolen Credit Cards
■ American Express (AE), www.americanexpress.com, 069 97 97 20 00
■ Diners Club (DC), www.dinersclub.com, 07531 363 31 11
■ MasterCard (MC), www.mastercard.com, 0800 819 10 40
■ Visa (V), www.visa.com, 0800 811 84 40

HOTELS

With more than 13 million visitors per year, Berlin boasts an adequate supply of accommodation: good news for tourists, because this excess capacity translates into rates well below those in other popular European capitals. This is a fairly compact city, so you should be able to find a hotel within a reasonable distance of the sights. Remember that Berlin is a major destination for its clubbing scene, and Berliners traditionally stay out long into the night, particularly on weekends, so you may prefer a room facing away from main roads. Many hotels accept all major cards, although some of the smaller ones take only cash.

TRAVEL ESSENTIALS

A spree of hotel-building has brought eastern Berlin largely up to standards in the west of the city. The central Mitte district boasts the lion's share of main draws such as the Museum Island art collections, and naturally it's the most popular area to stay. The old West can feel a bit staid, but there's refined charm in the squares and boutique-lined streets that feed into Kurfürstendamm (Ku'damm).

Before you book a room, it helps to make a personal checklist of must-have features such as elevators, air-conditioning, or a quiet location. Many hotels overlook busy streets, and not all have decent soundproofing.

If you're driving, know that many central hotels do not have their own parking and may direct you to a paid lot or garage nearby. Street parking may be tricky in built-up areas, although some establishments in the city issue permits.

In our listings, unless otherwise stated:
• Breakfast is not included in the price.
• All rooms have a telephone and television. Many hotels also provide Internet access, and Wi-Fi is usually standard.
• Room prices are a rough indicator and do not take seasonal variations or special offers into account.

Online Resources: A good starting point is www.visit berlin.de, run by the city's capable tourist authority, Berlin Tourismus & Kongress. The search pages show availability, special offers, location, features, and photos for more than 250 hotels, hostels, and B&Bs.

Price Range

An indication of the cost of a double room in the high season is given by € signs.
€€€€€ More than €200
€€€€ €150–€200
€€€ €100–€150
€€ €60–€100
€ Less than €60

Text Symbols

ⓘ No. of Guest Rooms
🚇 U-Bahn or S-Bahn 🅿 Parking
🛗 Elevator ❄ Air-conditioning
🚭 Nonsmoking 🏊 Outdoor Pool
🏊 Indoor Pool 💪 Health Club
💳 Credit Cards

Organization

Hotels listed here have been grouped first according to neighborhood, then listed alphabetically by price range.

UNTER DEN LINDEN & AROUND

Some of Berlin's most impressive luxury hotels are to be found in this neighborhood, as well as rooms for those on more modest budgets. This is a good location for all the major sights in central Berlin, including Potsdamer Platz with a range of attractions day and night. A number of these hotels are also perfectly placed for the government quarter and Tiergarten Park.

■ ADLON KEMPINSKI BERLIN

€€€€€
UNTER DEN LINDEN 77
TEL 030 22 610
www.kempinski.com
British club meets art deco at this portal of German history, where Marlene Dietrich was discovered and Joseph Goebbels chased his mistress down the corridor. The grand dame of Berlin hotels has been restored

to its pre-World War II splendor, complete with grandstand views of the Brandenburg Gate, not only from a number of the rooms, but also from terraced seating outside. The elegant Lorenz restaurant boasts three Michelin stars. All rooms have flatscreen TVs and Wi-Fi.

ℹ *382 + suites* **🚇** *S1, S2, U5 Brandenburger Tor* **P 🔁 🛗 🅂**
🖼 🍽 ⚡ *All major cards*

■ GRAND HYATT BERLIN
€€€€€
MARLENE-DIETRICH-PLATZ 2
TEL 030 25 53 12 34
berlin.grand.hyatt.com
A haunt of movie stars, celebrities, and the merely moneyed, this temple of luxury has matte black surfaces and carved cedarwood that exude a Euro-Japanese elegance. Rooms boast amenities such as heated bathroom floors and Bauhaus art. On the rooftop you'll find a gym, pool, and beauty center.

ℹ *342* **🚇** *S1, S2, U2 Potsdamer Platz* **P 🔁 🛗 🖼 🍽**
⚡ *All major cards*

■ RITZ-CARLTON BERLIN
€€€€€
POTSDAMER PLATZ 3
TEL 030 33 77 77
www.ritzcarlton.com
One of Berlin's premier luxury hotels, housed in a retro U.S.-style skyscraper with a hushed, columned lobby and sweeping staircase that harks back to the Prussian Empire. Rooms gleam with polished cherrywood, marble, and brass fittings. The Curtain Club serves signature cocktails in an

elegant atmosphere reminiscent of South America even in its live music, while indulging in afternoon tea is a must at The Lounge.

ℹ *303* **🚇** *S1, S2, U2 Potsdamer Platz* **P 🔁 🛗 🖼**
⚡ *All major cards*

■ MANDALA SUITES
€€€–€€€€
FRIEDRICHSTRASSE 185–190
TEL 030 20 29 20
www.themandalasuites.de
All manner of sophisticates frequent this ultra-discreet hideaway on Friedrichstrasse. If you want room service and bellboys go someplace else, but you'll miss being pampered in five categories of suite ranging from 430 to 1,100 square feet (40–100 sq m). Rooms have marble baths, walk-in closets, kitchen, and modern workspaces with Wi-Fi.

ℹ *80 suites* **🚇** *U2, U6 Stadtmitte* **P 🔁 🛗 🍽**
⚡ *All major cards*

■ NH COLLECTION BERLIN MITTE AM CHECKPOINT CHARLIE
€€€
LEIPZIGER STRASSE 106–111
TEL 030 20 37 60
www.nh-hotels.com
With its understated, linear elegance, it offers bright and spacious rooms and suites, some with pleasant balconies or facing the inner courtyard, for the ultimate in tranquility. Those traveling with children, or in a small group, will find the convenience of connecting rooms. There is an in-house

restaurant with German and Mediterranean cuisine, and the location is perfect for those who want to indulge not only in cultural sightseeing but also in shopping.

ℹ *392* **🚇** *U2, U6 Stadtmitte*
P 🔁 🛗 🅂 🍽
⚡ *All major cards*

AROUND MUSEUMSINSEL

This neighborhood offers a good range of hotels in the vibrant heart of the city. You won't improve on location when it comes to sightseeing: Museumsinsel, piers on the Spree River, and Alexanderplatz are all within minutes on foot. There are good shopping opportunities, too, at Friedrichstrasse and the Hackesche Höfe. This is, however, a busy district and can be noisy come nighttime.

■ CLASSIK HOTEL BERLIN ALEXANDER PLAZA
€€€–€€€€
ROSENSTRASSE 1
TEL 030 24 00 10
classik-hotel-collection.com
Housed in a stolid Bismarck-era monument that was once a furrier's studio, this hotel bristles with period details. The ergonomically designed rooms have soothing color schemes and panoramas of the historic quarter. Breakfast is served in the glass-covered Wintergarten.

ℹ *94* **🚇** *S3, S5, S7, S9 Hackescher Markt*
🔁 🛗 🍽 ⚡ *All major cards*

■ HONIGMOND GARDEN

€€€–€€€€

INVALIDENSTRASSE 122
TEL 030 28 44 55 77
www.honigmond.de

This romantic, family-run hotel transports you to 19th-century Berlin with original antiques, stucco ceilings, and polished wood floors. The rear chambers and kitchen-equipped cottages face an idyllic, shady garden with Japanese fishpond and century-old trees. Breakfast is included in the price.

ⓘ 16 **🚇** S1, S2 Nordbahnhof
Ⓟ Ⓢ 🏨 V, MC

■ MONBIJOU HOTEL

€€€–€€€€

MONBIJOUPLATZ 1
TEL 030 61 62 03 00
www.monbijouhotel.com

Steps from Hackescher Markt, this stylish boutique hotel features plush modern decor with hardwood floors, a well-stocked library, and large windows overlooking the Mitte neighborhood—some with views of Berliner Dom. There's a pleasant bar area and lounge with fireplace, and the Parisian-style bistro offers an international menu. In summer enjoy snacks and drinks on the rooftop terrace.

ⓘ 101 **🚇** S5, S7 Hackescher Markt **Ⓟ** (fee)**➋ Ⓢ**
🏨 All major cards

■ ARCOTEL VELVET

€€€

ORANIENBURGER STRASSE 52
TEL 030 278 75 30
www.arcotel.com

This stylish member of the Arcotel chain occupies a plum spot in Mitte, close

to the Neue Synagoge and Friedrichstrasse. Furnishings are sleek contemporary with dark hardwoods, red leather, and floor-to-ceiling windows. Flatscreen TVs and free room Wi-Fi are standard. Rooms on the upper floors offer fabulous views over the historic district. Breakfast is served in the fine Lutter & Wegner restaurant.

ⓘ 85 **🚇** U6 Oranienburger Tor
Ⓟ ➋ Ⓢ Ⓢ Ⓢ 🏨 All major cards

■ ARTE LUISE KUNSTHOTEL

€€€

LUISENSTRASSE 19
TEL 030 28 44 80
www.luise-berlin.com

Bedroom fantasy, you say? Each of the 50 rooms at this wacky art hotel is an installation designed by a young artist. Some play with your head (one has a ridiculously huge four-poster bed), draw on sci-fi (a Jetsons shower), or are chill (Japanese screens and Zen music). The location is convenient to the Reichstag, Unter den Linden, and the sights along Oranienburger Strasse. Rooms are tastefully appointed and quiet, apart from a few bedrooms next to the S-Bahn tracks.

ⓘ 50 **🚇** S1, S2, S3, S5, S7, S9, U6 Friedrichstrasse **➋ Ⓢ Ⓢ 🏨** All major cards

■ ART'OTEL BERLIN MITTE

€€€

WALLSTRASSE 70–73
TEL 030 24 06 20
www.radissonhotels.com

This rococo mansion, a

onetime haunt of Berlin's intellectual elite, is now a plush hotel cum art gallery. Spread over its six floors is a collection of works by modernist painter Georg Baselitz. You can dine in the glass-roofed Factory restaurant or outside on the banks of the Spree River.

ⓘ 105 **🚇** U2 Märkisches Museum **Ⓟ ➋ Ⓢ Ⓢ 🏨**
🏨 All major cards

■ CLASSIK HOTEL BERLIN HACKESCHER MARKT

€€€

GROSSE PRÄSIDENTENSTRASSE 8
TEL 030 28 00 30
classik-hotel-collection.com

In a nicely renovated 19th-century town house, this urbane hotel is perfectly situated for tapping the nightlife around Hackescher Markt. The rooms and suites have pleasant country-style furnishings and floor heating in the bathrooms. Most quarters face a peaceful green courtyard, and some even have balconies. The English-speaking staff are eager to help. Although some rooms are snug, you can't quibble with the location.

ⓘ 31 **🚇** S3, S5, S7, S9 Hackescher Markt
Ⓟ ➋ Ⓢ 🏨 All major cards

■ THE DUDE BY CHARLY

€€€

KÖPENICKER STRASSE 92
TEL 030 41 19 88 100
www.thedudeberlin.com

Housed in one of historic Berlin's oldest surviving buildings (1822), this designer

hotel exudes an atmosphere of staying in one's own private luxury residence. The hotel has a range of rooms with flawless attention to detail and exquisite modern furniture. Features include a cigar lounge and the in-house restaurant, The Brooklyn, is renowned for its steaks and 160 rare whiskies.
🚹 30 🚇 U2 Märkisches Museum
🅿 🚫 ♿ All major cards

■ INDIGO BERLIN KU'DAMM
€€€
HARDENBERGSTRASSE 15
TEL 030 86 09 090
www.ihg.com/hotelindigo
Located just a few minutes' walk north of Alexanderplatz, this new and affordable hotel is a good home base for exploring central Berlin. The rooms are small but crisply clean and modern, and excellent service is provided by a friendly, youthful staff. Other amenities include a large and welcoming bar, free Wi-Fi, in-room coffee machines, and a well-appointed gym.
🚹 153 🚇 S3, S5, S7, S9, U2, U5, U8 Alexanderplatz 🅿 (in vicinity)
🔄 🚭 🖥 ♿ All major cards

■ LUX ELEVEN
€€€
ROSA-LUXEMBURG-STRASSE 11–13
TEL 030 936 28 00
www.lux-eleven.com
A haunt of pencil-thin fashion models and media types, these spacious apartments were once used by visitors to the dreaded Ministry of

State Security. They are now done up in a minimalist Far Eastern style. Soft cuddly things abound—pillows, comfy chairs, piles of towels—to make spaces plush and inviting. Rooms boast Wi-Fi and flatscreen TVs. Guests here can plug into the gallery scene of Mitte or just retreat to their personal cocoons.
🚹 72 apts. 🚇 S3, S5, S7, S9, U2, U5, U8 Alexanderplatz
🅿 🔄 🚭 🖥 ♿ All major cards

■ RADISSON COLLECTION HOTEL BERLIN
€€€
KARL-LIEBKNECHT-STRASSE 3
TEL 030 23 82 80
www.radissonhotels.com
The Radisson's main feature is its enormous cylindrical aquarium: Most guests fall under its Jules Verne spell right away. The most impressive rooms face either the towering tank in the courtyard or overlook the Spree River and majestic Berlin Cathedral. Flatscreen TVs and free Wi-Fi are standard. All guests get a free riverboat tour, and for those with energy to burn, the fitness room is open 24 hours.
🚹 427 🚇 U5 Rotes Rathaus
🅿 🔄 🚫 🛗 🖥
♿ All major cards

■ THE CIRCUS HOTEL
€€–€€€
ROSENTHALER STRASSE 1
TEL 030 20 00 39 39
www.circus-berlin.de
The Circus is handily situated on Rosenthaler Platz in the

hub of the Mitte district. The garden courtyard (and rear quarters overlooking it) are a great place to relax, and there are hip little amenities such as loudspeakers loaded with music. Rooms are clean, stylish, and colorful. There's Wi-Fi throughout, and all of the rooms have laptop safes.
🚹 60 🚇 U8 Rosenthaler Platz
🔄 🚭 🚫 ♿ All major cards

■ NEUER FRITZ
€€–€€€
FRIEDRICHSTRASSE 105
TEL 030 28 49 00
www.neuerfritz.com
Behind its bland communist-era facade, you'll be surprised by a young and pleasantly colorful atmosphere. There are rooms to suit all budgets, from suites to standard doubles and even "size XS," for very short, economy stays, all furnished in a modern and original way. The restaurant offers Italian-inspired cuisine and pizzas, with outdoor seating along the river.
🚹 40 🚇 S1, S2, S3, S5, S7, S9, U6 Friedrichstrasse 🅿 🔄 🚫
♿ All major cards

■ MIDI INN PARKHOTEL MITTE
€€
VETERANENSTRASSE 10
TEL 030 91 48 81 97
www.midi-inn.de
This stylish boutique hotel has an enviable location—overlooking the rolling Weinbergspark, on the cusp of sight-filled Mitte and hip Prenzlauer Berg. Though on the cozy side, the double

rooms have huge windows, smart designs, and attractive canvases by a London artist. Management rents out several fine apartments close by. Breakfast is served in the restaurant-bar.

i 3 + 4 apts. **⊞** U8 Rosenthaler Platz **⊟** ⓢ ⓐ AE, MC, V

■ **PFEFFERBETT HOSTEL**
€–€€
CHRISTINENSTRASSE 18–19
TEL 030 93 93 58 58
pfefferbett.de
The 19th-century brick building was a brewery for many years. Today it is part of a complex with a theater, restaurant and workshops, a haunt of young, creative people. There are 7 types of rooms with different capacities (single to 8 people), with en suite or shared bathroom, but all have TV and internet connection via WLAN. Bike and scooter rental available.

i 45 **⊞** U2 Senefelderplatz **⊟** ⓢ ⓐ All major cards

TIERGARTEN & AROUND

This is one of Berlin's quieter neighborhoods. Hotels here are perfectly placed for visiting the government quarter and, of course, Berlin's green lung, Tiergarten Park. A number of hotels are also within walking distance of the Kulturforum to the south of the park, for art galleries by day and the Berlin Philharmonie by night.

■ **SO/ BERLIN DAS STUE**
€€€€€
DRAKESTRASSE 1
TEL 030 31 17 22 0
www.so-berlin-das-stue.com
Claiming to be Berlin's first luxury boutique hotel, Das Stue nestles in lush Tiergarten park, close to Berlin's zoological gardens. The handsome 1930s building—originally the Danish Embassy—has been remodeled within by Spanish architect Patricia Urquiola. The generous rooms are luxurious and come with all modern comforts, including free Wi-Fi. The hotel has two restaurants, one of which (Cinco) is Michelin-starred.

i 70 **⊞** S3, S5, S7, S9 Tiergarten **P** **⊟** ⓢ ⓐ ⓥ ⓐ All major cards

■ **ABION SPREEBOGEN WATERSIDE**
€€€
ALT-MOABIT 99
TEL 030 39 92 00
ameroncollection.com
Towering above the Spree River north of Tiergarten park, this hotel is housed in a former dairy farm. With its own landing pier right outside, the hotel runs a number of river cruises. There are several well-appointed family rooms and suites available. You'll pay more for a riverside room, but the views are worth it. Additional features include an in-house restaurant, bicycle rental, and free Wi-Fi.

i 243 **⊞** U9 Turmstrasse **P** **⊟** ⓢ ⓥ ⓐ All major cards

■ **BERLIN, BERLIN**
€€–€€€
LÜTZOWPLATZ 17
TEL 030 26 050
www.hotel-berlin.de
Host to many a business conference, this cavernous hotel has more than 500 rooms, yet manages to feel warm and personal. During the Cold War, visiting celebrities and politicians often stayed here, and staff are full of anecdotes of the era. The rooms are immense, modern, and spotless. Wi-Fi is free throughout the hotel, and breakfast is included.

i 500 **⊞** U1, U2, U3, U4 Nollendorfplatz **P** **⊟** ⓢ ⓥ ⓐ All major cards

CHARLOTTENBURG

This well-established neighborhood was the hub of West Berlin during the Cold War. It is the ideal location from which to visit Charlottenburg Palace and remains one of Berlin's principle shopping districts. Hotels here are good value for money on the whole, and there are plenty of restaurants to choose from in the streets around Savignyplatz, Breitscheidplatz, and Kurfürstendamm.

■ **HOTEL AM STEINPLATZ**
€€€€–€€€€€
STEINPLATZ 4
TEL 030 55 44 440
www.hotelsteinplatz.com
Reopened in 2013, it saw its height during Berlin's golden

years. Its rooms boast having hosted Vladimir Nabokov and Brigitte Bardot, among others. The turn-of-the-century atmosphere and elegance are still palpable and the hospitality is excellent.

ⓘ 87 🚇 S3, S5, S7, S9, U2, U9 Zoologischer Garten **P** ⊜ 🍸

⛎ All major cards

■ **BIKINI 25 HOURS**
€€€–€€€€
BUDAPESTER STRASSE 40
TEL 030 12 02 210
www.25hours-hotels.com
This hotel is arguably Berlin's hippest new arrival. With "urban jungle" as its theme, the hotel's rooms are divided into those that look out across the city (Urban) and those that overlook the ape house at Berlin's zoo (Jungle). The hotel also boasts a wood-fire bakery, sauna, and roof terrace with views across Tiergarten park. Free bike rental and Wi-Fi come standard with every room.

ⓘ 149 🚇 S3, S5, S7, S9, U2, U9 Zoologischer Garten **P** ⊜ 🄢

⛎ All major cards

■ **Q!**
€€€–€€€€
KNESEBECKSTRASSE 67
TEL 030 810 06 60
www.hotel-q.com
A cool gray facade signals your arrival at the Q!, named for nearby Ku'damm. This hotel smoothes out the rough edges by eliminating corners. Hardwood floors curve up the walls in the rooms, where you can literally slide from the tub into bed. The spa has its own self-contained beach with heated sand, aromatherapy, and sound and light effects.

ⓘ 77 🚇 S3, S5, S7, S9 Savignyplatz **P** 🄢 🍸

⛎ All major cards

■ **DORMERO HOTEL BERLIN KU'DAMM**
€€€
EISLEBENER STRASSE 14
TEL 030 21 40 50
www.dormero.de /hotel-berlin-kudamm
Bauhaus- and modern design make this elegant early 20th-century villa a hotel with an atmosphere like few others. The airy, light-filled rooms are tastefully furnished, with very high ceilings. The restaurant, Die Quadriga, one of the best in town, serves only fine German wines.

ⓘ 72 🚇 U2, U3 Augsburger Strasse **P** ⊜ 🄢 🍸

⛎ All major cards

■ **HECKER'S**
€€€
GROLMANSTRASSE 35
TEL 030 889 00
www.heckers-hotel.de
Just a few steps off busy Kurfürstendamm, this renowned boutique hotel prides itself on the personal service it heaps on celebrities that have included Michael Douglas, Valéry Giscard d'Estaing, and a bunch of rock stars. The huge, elegant quarters range from Bauhaus to Italo-chic. The lobby has a striking ice blue backlit bar.

ⓘ 69 🚇 S3, S5, S7, S9 Savignyplatz; U1 Uhlandstrasse **P** ⊜ 🄢 🄢 ⛎ All major cards

■ **KU'DAMM 101**
€€€
KURFÜRSTENDAMM 101
TEL 030 520 05 50
www.kudamm101.com
A bit removed from the action, this hotel is fascinating viewing for anyone with an eye for minimalist design. The lobby combines 1960s design with New Age—column lamps, curvy banquettes, and recessed ceilings. The rooms are a clever blend of light and shadow. There's high-speed Internet and retro touches like a wood-grain console that hides the TV.

ⓘ 170 🚇 S41, S42, S46 Halensee **P** ⊜ 🄢

⛎ All major cards

■ **PROVOCATEUR BERLIN**
€€€
BRANDENBURGISCHE STRASSE 21
TEL 030 22 05 60 60
www.provocateur-hotel.com
The name speaks for itself. Bold design here is unafraid of excess and opulence, in a 1920s style meant to be Parisian, with furnishings that take advantage of deep hues and velvet. Class, comfort, perfect location for shopping and nightlife, and burlesque shows in the cocktail bar. The Golden Phoenix restaurant serves fine French and Chinese-inspired cuisine.

ⓘ 58 🚇 U7 Konstanzer Strasse ⊜ 🄢 ⛎ All major cards

■ **BLEIBTREU**
€€–€€€
BLEIBTREUSTRASSE 31
TEL 030 88 47 40
www.goldentulip.com

HOTELS

The cheery, ecofriendly materials and minimalist Italian furniture of this boutique hotel are completely in step with the fancy apparel shops along Bleibtreustrasse. Some of the rooms are on the tight side, but the in-house bar and Restaurant 31 are quite elegant.

(i) 60 **[R]** S3, S5, S7, S9 Savignyplatz **[P]** **[≡]** **[S]** **[Y]**
[◈] All major cards

■ MIDI INN CITY WEST
€€–€€€
WIELANDSTRASSE 26
TEL 030 88 91 72 52
kudamm-de.midi-inn.de
A guesthouse, recently renovated, on the third floor of a period building. You can feel the air of old Berlin here: high stucco-decorated ceilings and old lithographs, plus a breakfast room with antique sideboards.

(i) 22 **[R]** S3, S5, S7, S9 Savignyplatz **[P]** **[≡]** **[S]**
[◈] No carte di credito

BERLIN'S EAST

Berlin's eastern districts offer accommodations in the leafy residential streets of Prenzlauer Berg as well as close proximity to the clubbing scene in Friedrichshain. The area has a relatively laid-back vibe with a lively café and restaurant scene. However, with the exception of the Berlin Wall Memorial and the East Side Gallery, none of the city's major sights are in this area.

■ ADELE
€€€
GREIFSWALDER STRASSE 227
TEL 030 44 32 43 10
adele-berlin.de
From the street, this lounge hotel is cleverly camouflaged by a row of coffee and wine shops. Rooms look like something out of *Wallpaper* magazine, with dark hardwoods and leathers set off by cream and pastel hues. There's a fine Mediterranean-inspired restaurant.

(i) 14 **[R]** U2 Senefelderplatz **[P]** **[≡]** **[S]** **[◈]** All major cards

■ KASTANIENHOF
€€€
KASTANIENALLEE 65
TEL 030 44 30 50
www.kastanienhof.berlin
This guesthouse has a great location on Kastanienallee, a hip nightlife strip in Prenzlauer Berg. The historic building hosted a butcher shop, Russian military post, and tenements before being turned into one of East Berlin's first hotels after reunification. The furnishings are simple, but the historic maps and photos in the rooms ooze atmosphere.

(i) 35 **[R]** U8 Rosenthaler Platz
[P] **[≡]** **[S]** **[◈]** All major cards

■ NHOW BERLIN
€€€
STRALAUER ALLEE 3
TEL 030 290 29 90
www.nhow-hotels.com
Flash Gordon meets Barbie at this "music lifestyle hotel" lodged in a converted riverside granary. Futuristic shapes and bubblegum colors are

dominant themes. All rooms are equipped with Wi-Fi, iPod dock, and flatscreen IP-TVs that double as mirrors. The stainless-steel tower has a number of music studios for rent; room service will even send up a Gibson guitar with headphones.

(i) 304 **[R]** S3, S5, S7, S9, U1 Warschauer Strasse **[P]** **[≡]** **[S]** **[◈]**
[Y] **[◈]** All major cards

■ MICHELBERGER
€€–€€€
WARSCHAUER STRASSE 39–40
TEL 030 29 77 85 90
www.michelbergerhotel.com
An old warehouse reborn as a hotel, the Michelberger pitches affordable charms for night owls in buzzing Friedrichshain. The interiors of this budget boutique hotel are kept raw with exposed wiring, feature playful touches like raised beds, and have free Wi-Fi. The laid-back bar area has comfy sofas and a travel library that is well worth a browse. This hotel is within easy walking distance of some of Europe's best nightclubs, including Berghain.

(i) 119 **[R]** S3, S5, S7, S9, U1 Warschauer Strasse **[≡]** **[S]**
[◈] MC, V

■ ALTE-BÄCKEREI-PANKOW
€€
WOLLANKSTRASSE 130
TEL 030 48 64 669
www.alte-baeckerei-pankow.de
This has to be one of the quaintest places to stay in Berlin. Occupying the attic rooms of an old bakery, this

hostel sleeps just 2 people. With rustic furnishings throughout, it's reminiscent of scenes from Hansel and Gretel or Goldilocks. Also on the premises are a museum of childhood and a fully operational bakery, producing rustic-looking bread (3–6 p.m., Tues., Wed., Fri.).

(i) 1 **(train)** S1, S2 Wollankstrasse **P (S) (bike)** No credit cards

■ OLD TOWN HOTEL
€€
GREIFSWALDER STRASSE 211
TEL 030 54 71 38 90
www.ota-berlin.de
Perhaps not highly original in design, but pleasant, each room is unique, colorful and cozy. Double and triple rooms are available, and the common areas are bright and comfortable; breakfast is served in the inner courtyard, adorned with flowers and plants. The location is convenient for enjoying Prenzlauer Berg and its vibrancy.

(i) 24 **(train)** U2 Senefelderplatz **(S) (S)** All major cards

■ 26 BERLIN
€€
GRÜNBERGER STRASSE 26
TEL 030 297 77 80
www.hotel26-berlin.de
For no-nonsense digs a cut above a hostel, try this small, eco-friendly hotel in the go-ahead Friedrichshain district. Breakfast (included) is a magnificent organic spread of cheeses, fresh juices, and cold cuts. You can chill in the pleasant café or catch some rays on the lounge chairs in the rear garden.

(i) 19 **(train)** U5 Frankfurter Tor **P (S) (S)** All major cards

■ SUNFLOWER HOSTEL
€–€€
HELSINGFORSER STRASSE 17
TEL 030 44 04 42 50
www.sunflower-hostel.de
A nice place to stay in the city and enjoy sights and attractions, as well as some Berlin nightlife, given the friendly prices and location within walking distance of Raw Tempel, Urban Spree, and East Side Gallery. Rooms have different capacities, from single, to dormitory, to self-catering accommodation. All are nicely and colorfully furnished. The hostel offers many services such as laundry facilities, an all-day bar, breakfast served late, and bike rental.

(i) 42 **(train)** S3, S5, S7, S9, U1 Warschauer Strasse **(S)** All major cards

SCHÖNEBERG & KREUZBERG

With a sprinkling of sights that include the Jüdisches Museum, the Berlinische Galerie, and the Landwehrkanal, these neighborhoods combine the quiet, leafy streets of bohemian Schöneberg with the more multicultual, edgy vibe of Kreuzberg and Kottbusser Tor. Now stretching toward up-and-coming Neukölln, this district has plenty of good-value accommodations and a rich and varied nightlife.

■ MÖVENPICK HOTEL BERLIN
€€€
SCHÖNEBERGER STRASSE 3
TEL 030 23 00 60
www.movenpick.com
Once the headquarters of electronics giant Siemens, this hotel south of Potsdamer Platz offers funky design in a historic shell. The lounge bar is made of high-voltage equipment, and old turbines are displayed in the halls. Other highlights are the glass-bricked bathrooms, olivewood, and perky colors recalling Möevenpick ice cream.

(i) 243 **(train)** S1, S2 Anhalter Bahnhof **P (S) (S) (S) (S)** **(S)** All major cards

■ HÜTTENPALAST BERLIN
€€–€€€
HOBRECHTSTRASSE 66
TEL 030 37 30 58 06
www.huettenpalast.de
Indoor "glamping" is the draw at this old vacuum cleaner factory. Artists have redesigned three vintage camping trailers and three huts for guests. Relax in the garden under fake trees. An organic breakfast (included) is served in the courtyard café. Regular rooms with en suite bathrooms are available in the rear wing.

(i) 19 **(train)** U7, U8 Hermannplatz

■ PARK PLAZA WALL STREET
€€–€€€
WALLSTRASSE 23–24
TEL 030 847 11 70
www.radissonhotels.com

This deluxe four-star hotel near Checkpoint Charlie is something of a capitalist send-up, with dollar bills and stock-ticker symbols printed on carpets and drapes. The quarters are plush and state of the art. The well-appointed rooms are packed with quality woods, textiles, and perks like free Wi-Fi, a flatscreen TV, and a laptop safe.

⑪ *80* **🚇** *U2 Märkisches Museum* **🅿 🔁 🔇 🔇 🔊**
🃏 *All major cards*

■ GRAND HOSTEL CLASSIC

€–€€
TEMPELHOFER UFER 14
TEL 030 20 09 54 50
grandhostel-berlin.de

The setting is that of a grand hotel, but in reality it is a modern hostel. The rooms in this 19th-century building, with high ceilings, parquet floors, and elegant decorative elements, have become private rooms and multi-bed dorms. Also: bike rental, tours, bar, and various activities (even German lessons!).

⑪ *35* **🚇** *U1, U3, U7 Möckernbrücke* **🔁 🔇**
🃏 *All major cards*

DAHLEM & THE WEST

Merely a fifteen-minute ride to central Berlin on the S-Bahn, this neighborhood feels a world apart from the inner city. You'll find exceptional value for money and simple comfort in streets lined with 19th-century villas. Close proximity to Grunewald, the Museum Europäischer Kulturen, and Berlin's botanical gardens.

■ FRIEDENAU – DAS LITERATURHOTEL BERLIN

€€€
FREGESTRASSE 68
TEL 030 85 90 96 0
www.literaturhotel-berlin.de

This elegant 19th-century villa is furnished in the German Biedermeier style. At the heart of the hotel is a room dedicated to the area's literary heroes, with books, biographies, manuscripts, drawings, and photos. In summer, you can breakfast in the dappled shade of the garden to the rear of the hotel (breakfast included).

⑪ *18* **🚊** *S1 Friedenau* **🔁 🃏** *V, MC*

■ ANNA 1908

€€
BÜSINGSTRASSE 1
TEL 030 99 40 45 20
lindemannhotels.de

A nice, unpretentious hotel housed in a period building. Although not exactly central, public transportation is near and very efficient A healthy, fresh breakfast is included, and there is also parking available for a small fee.

⑪ *46* **🚊** *S1 Friedenau* **🅿 🔁 🔇 🔇 🃏** *All major cards*

LANGUAGE **GUIDE**

In German "ss" can also be written as "ß." Called a "sharp s," you will see this construction in many words, such as *Straße* (street). It is pronounced in exactly the same way as "ss."

Useful Words & Phrases
Yes *Ja*
No *Nein*
Please *Bitte*
Thank you *Danke*
Excuse me *Entschuldigen Sie bitte*
Goodbye *Auf Wiedersehen*
Good morning *Guten Morgen*
Good day (afternoon) *Guten Tag*
Good evening *Guten Abend*
Good night *Gute Nacht*
today *heute*
yesterday *gestern*
tomorrow *morgen*
now *jetzt*
later *später*
left *links*
right *rechts*
straight ahead *geradeaus*
Do you speak English? *Sprechen Sie Englisch?*
I am American *Ich bin Amerikaner (m)/ Amerikanerin (f)*
I don't understand *Ich verstehe Sie nicht*
Where is/are...? *Wo ist/sind...?*
My name is... *Ich heisse...*
At what time? *Wann?*
What time is it? *Wie viel Uhr ist es?*

In the Hotel
Do you have a vacancy? *Haben Sie noch ein Zimmer frei?*
a single room *ein Einzelzimmer*
a double room *ein Doppelzimmer*
with/without bathroom/ shower *mit/ohne Bad/Dusche*

Emergencies
Help *Hilfe*
I need a doctor/dentist *Bitte rufen Sie einen Arzt/Zahnarzt*
Can you help me? *Können Sie mir helfen?*
Where is the hospital?/police station?/telephone? *Wo finde ich das Krankenhaus?/die Polizeiwache?/das Telefon?*

Shopping
Do you have...? *Haben Sie...?*
How much is it? *Wie viel kostet es?*
Do you take credit cards *Akzeptieren Sie Kreditkarten?*
When do you open/close? *Wann machen Sie auf/zu?*
size (clothes) *Kleidergrösse*
size (shoes) *Schuhgrösse*
small change *Kleingeld*
cheap *billig*
expensive *teuer*

Sightseeing
visitor information *Touristen- Information*
exhibition *Ausstellung*
open *geöffnet*
closed *geschlossen*
entry fee *Eintrittspreis*

Menu Reader
I'd like to order *Ich möchte bestellen*
I am a vegetarian *Ich bin Vegetarier (m)/Vegetarierin (f)*
The check, please *Die Rechnung, bitte*
dinner *Abendessen*
menu *Speisekarte*

salt *Salz*
pepper *Pfeffer*
bread *Brot*
cheese *Käse*
wine list *Weinkarte*
water *Wasser*

Drinks *Getränke*
Apfelsaft apple juice
Bier beer
Kaffee coffee
Orangensaft orange juice
Rotwein red wine
Weisswein white wine

Breakfast *Frühstück*
Brötchen bread roll
Eier eggs
Speck bacon

Meat & Fish *Fleisch & Fisch*
Bockwurst large frankfurter
Forelle trout
Krabben shrimp
Lachs salmon
Leberknödel liver dumplings
Rinderbraten roast beef
Sauerbraten marinated beef
Schinken ham

Fruit & Vegetables *Obst & Gemüse*
Apfel apple
Apfelsine/Orange orange
Erdbeeren strawberries
Kartoffeln potatoes
Kohl cabbage
Reis rice
Spargel asparagus
Weintrauben grapes
Zitrone lemon
Zwiebeln onions

Desserts *Nachspeisen*
Apfelkuchen apple cake
Krapfen/Berliner doughnuts
Obstkuchen fruit tart

INDEX

INDEX

CREDITS

Walking Berlin
Paul Sullivan

Since 1888, the National Geographic Society has funded more than 14,000 research, conservation, education, and storytelling projects around the world. National Geographic Partners distributes a portion of the funds it receives from your purchase to National Geographic Society to support programs including the conservation of animals and their habitats.

National Geographic Partners, LLC
1145 17th Street NW
Washington, DC 20036-4688 USA

Get closer to National Geographic explorers and photographers, and connect with our global community. Join us today at nationalgeographic.org/joinus

For rights or permissions inquiries, please contact National Geographic Books Subsidiary Rights: bookrights@natgeo.com

Edition edited by White Star s.r.l.
Licensee of National Geographic Partners, LLC.
Update by Iceigeo, Milan (Ilaria Ghisletti, Alexa Ahern)

The information in this book has been carefully checked and to the best of our knowledge is accurate. However, details are subject to change, and the publisher cannot be responsible for such changes, or for errors or omissions. Assessments of sites, hotels, and restaurants are based on the author's subjective opinions, which do not necessarily reflect the publisher's opinion.

ISBN: 978-8-8544-1967-4

Printed In China
23/TL/1

MIX
Paper from
responsible sources
FSC® C178000
www.fsc.org